cook's library
Chicken

cook's library
Chicken

p

This is a Parragon Book
This edition published in 2003

Parragon
Queen Street House
4 Queen Street
Bath BA1 1HE, UK

ISBN: 0-75258 750 1

Printed in China

NOTE

This book uses metric and imperial measurements. Follow the same
units of measurement throughout; do not mix metric and imperial.
All spoon measurements are level: teaspoons are assumed to be 5 ml,
and tablespoons are assumed to be 15 ml. Unless otherwise stated,
milk is assumed to be full fat, eggs and individual vegetables such as
potatoes are medium, and pepper is freshly ground black pepper.

The times given for each recipe are an approximate guide only because the
preparation times may differ according to the techniques used by different
people and the cooking times may vary as a result of the type of oven used.
The preparation times include chilling and marinating times, where appropriate.

Recipes using raw or very lightly cooked eggs should be
avoided by infants, the elderly, pregnant women, convalescents,
and anyone suffering from an illness.

Contents

Introduction

Chicken has become justly popular around the world and plays an important part in our modern diet, being reasonably priced and nutritionally sound. A versatile meat, it lends itself to an enormous range of cooking methods and cuisines. Its unassertive flavour means that it is equally suited to both sweet and savoury dishes.

Since it has a low fat content, especially without the skin, chicken is an ideal meat for low cholesterol and calorie-controlled diets. As well as being an excellent source of protein, it contains valuable minerals, such as potassium and phosphorus, and a number of the important B vitamins.

The recipes included in this book come from many countries and cultures. Grouped into sections, they reflect the wonderful versatility of chicken. There are recipes for warming, wholesome chicken soups, simple snacks and appetizers, slow-cooked casseroles, tempting roast meals, low-fat stir-fries, mouthwatering grills and barbecues, and fragrant spicy dishes.

Trying out new recipes, even with familiar ingredients, is fun and a great way to encourage healthier eating. For great results every time, follow the information on the next pages explaining the different cooking techniques, as well as the advice on storing, handling and preparing raw chicken. Take advantage, too, of the section of recipes for basic stocks and other essential ingredients needed for many of the main dishes.

Cooking techniques

Roasting

To prepare a chicken for roasting, remove any fat from the body cavity. Rinse the bird inside and out with water, then pat dry with kitchen paper. Season the cavity generously with salt and pepper and add stuffing, herbs or lemon, if wished. Spread the breast of the chicken with softened butter or oil. Place on a rack in a roasting tin or shallow baking dish. Roast the bird, basting two or three times with the pan juices during roasting. If the chicken browns too quickly, cover it with foil. Use a meat thermometer or insert a skewer into the thickest part of the thigh to see if the meat is ready. If the chicken is cooked, the juices will run clear with no trace of pink. Put the bird on a carving board and leave to rest for 15 minutes before serving. Make a sauce or a gravy from the juices left in the roasting tin.

Grilling

The intense heat of the grill quickly seals the succulent flesh of the chicken beneath a crisp, golden exterior. Place the chicken 10–15 cm/4–6 inches away from a moderate heat source. If the chicken seems to be browning too quickly, reduce the heat slightly. If the chicken is grilled at too high a temperature too near to the heat, the outside will burn before the inside is cooked. If it is cooked for too long under a low heat, it will dry out. Divide the chicken into joints to ensure even cooking. Breast meat, if cooked in one piece, can be rather dry, so it is best to cut it into chunks for kebabs. Wings are the best cut for speedy grilling.

Frying

This method of cooking is suitable for small thighs, drumsticks and joints. Dry the chicken pieces with kitchen paper so that they brown properly and to prevent spitting during cooking. The chicken can be coated in seasoned flour, egg and breadcrumbs or a batter. Heat the oil or a mixture of oil and butter in a deep frying pan. When the oil is very hot, add the chicken pieces, skin-side down. Fry until deep golden brown all over, turning the pieces frequently during cooking. Drain well on kitchen paper before serving.

Sautéing

Ideal for small pieces or small birds. Heat a little oil or oil and butter in a heavy-based frying pan. Add the chicken and fry over a moderate heat until golden, turning frequently. Add stock or other liquid, bring to the boil, cover and reduce the heat. Cook gently until the chicken is cooked through.

Stir-frying

This is perfect for skinless, boneless equal-sized pieces to ensure that the meat cooks evenly and stays succulent. Preheat a wok or frying pan before adding a small amount of oil. When the oil starts to smoke, add the chicken and stir-fry for 3–4 minutes, until cooked through. Other ingredients can be cooked at the same time, or the chicken can be cooked by itself, then removed from the pan while you stir-fry the remaining ingredients.

Casseroling

Good for slow cooking joints from larger, more mature chickens, or cooking whole smaller chickens, producing tender, flavoursome meat. Brown the chicken in butter or oil, or both. Add stock, wine or a mixture with seasoning and herbs, cover and cook on top of the hob or in the oven until the chicken is tender. Add lightly sautéed vegetables about halfway through the cooking time.

Braising

Chicken pieces or a small whole chicken and vegetables are cooked together slowly in a low oven. Heat oil in an ovenproof, flameproof casserole and gently fry the chicken until golden. Remove and fry the vegetables until they are almost tender. Replace the chicken, cover tightly and cook very gently on the top of the stove or in a low oven.

Poaching

A gentle cooking method that produces tender chicken and a stock that can be used to make a sauce to serve with the chicken. Put a whole chicken, bouquet garni, leek, carrot and onion in a large, flameproof casserole. Cover with water, season with salt and pepper and bring to the boil. Reduce the heat, simmer for 1½–2 hours until the chicken is tender. Lift out the chicken, discard the bouquet garni and use the stock to make a sauce. Blend the vegetables to thicken the stock and serve with the chicken.

Food Safety & Tips

When storing, handling and preparing poultry, certain precautions must be observed to prevent the possibility of food poisoning, since chicken can become contaminated by salmonella bacteria.

- Check the sell-by date and best before date. After buying, take the chicken home quickly, preferably in a freezer bag or cool box.

- Put frozen birds in the freezer immediately.

- If storing in the refrigerator, remove the wrappings and store any giblets separately. Place the chicken in a shallow dish to catch any drips. Cover loosely with foil and store on the bottom shelf of the refrigerator for no more than two or three days, depending on the best before date. Avoid any contact between raw chicken and cooked food during storage and preparation. Wash your hands thoroughly after handling raw chicken.

- Prepare raw chicken on a chopping board that can be easily cleaned and bleached, such as a non-porous, plastic board.

- Frozen birds should be defrosted before cooking. If time permits, defrost for about 36 hours in the refrigerator, or thaw for about 12 hours in a cool place. Bacteria breed in warm food at room temperature and when chicken is thawing. Cooking at high temperatures kills bacteria. There should be no ice crystals and the flesh should feel soft and flexible. Cook the chicken as soon as possible after thawing.

- Make sure that the chicken is cooked. Test if the chicken is done using a meat thermometer – the thigh should reach at least 79°C/175°F when cooked. Otherwise, pierce the thickest part of the thigh with a skewer – the juices should run clear, not pink or red. Never partially cook chicken with the intention of completing the cooking later.

Basic Recipes

These recipes form the basis of several of the dishes contained in this book. Many of these basic recipes can be made in advance and stored in the refrigerator until required.

Fresh Chicken Stock

MAKES
1.75 LITRES/3 PINTS

1 kg/2 lb 4 oz chicken, skinned
2 celery sticks, chopped
1 onion, sliced
2 carrots, chopped
1 garlic clove
few sprigs of fresh parsley
2 litres/3½ pints water
salt and pepper

1 Place the ingredients in a large saucepan and bring to the boil.

2 Skim away surface scum using a large flat spoon. Reduce the heat to a gentle simmer, partially cover, and cook for 2 hours. Leave to cool.

3 Line a sieve with clean muslin and place it over a large jug or bowl. Pour the stock through the sieve. The cooked chicken can be used in another recipe. Discard the other solids. Cover the stock and chill.

4 Skim away any fat that forms on the top. Cover the stock and store in the refrigerator for up to 3 days, until required, or freeze in small batches for later use.

Fresh Vegetable Stock

MAKES
1.75 LITRES/3 PINTS

1 large onion, sliced
1 large carrot, diced
1 celery stick, chopped
2 garlic cloves
1 dried bay leaf
few sprigs of fresh parsley
pinch of grated nutmeg
2 litres/3½ pints water
salt and pepper

1 Place the ingredients in a large saucepan and bring to the boil.

2 Skim away surface scum using a large flat spoon. Reduce the heat to a gentle simmer, partially cover, and cook for 45 minutes. Leave to cool.

3 Line a sieve with clean muslin and place over a large jug or bowl. Pour the stock through the sieve. Discard the solids.

4 Cover the stock and store in the refrigerator for up to 3 days until required, or freeze in small batches for later use.

Cornflour Paste

Mix 1 part cornflour with about 1.5 parts of cold water. Stir until smooth. The paste can be used to thicken sauces.

Fresh Bouquet Garni

1 fresh or dried bay leaf
few sprigs of fresh parsley
few sprigs of fresh thyme

Tie the herbs together with a length of string or cotton.

Dried Bouquet Garni

1 dried bay leaf
good pinch of dried mixed herbs or any one herb
good pinch of dried parsley
8–10 black peppercorns
2–4 cloves
1 garlic clove (optional)

Put the ingredients in a small square of muslin and secure with string or cotton, leaving a long tail so it can be tied to the handle of the pan for easy removal.

Chinese Stock

MAKES
2.5 LITRES/4½ PINTS

750 g/1 lb 10 oz chicken pieces, trimmed
    and chopped
750 g/1 lb 10 oz pork spare ribs, trimmed
    and chopped
3.75 litres/6 pints cold water
3–4 pieces of fresh root ginger, chopped
3–4 spring onions, each tied into a knot
3–4 tbsp Chinese rice wine or dry sherry

1 Place the chicken and pork in a
   large saucepan with the water.
   Add the ginger and spring onions.

2 Bring to the boil, and skim off any
   scum with a large flat spoon.
   Reduce the heat and simmer,
   uncovered, for at least 2–3 hours.

3 Strain the stock, discarding the
   chicken, pork, ginger and spring
   onions. Add the Chinese rice wine
   and return to the boil. Reduce the
   heat and simmer for 2–3 minutes.
   Leave to cool.

4 Cover the stock and store in the
   refrigerator for up to 5 days, until
   required, or freeze in small
   batches for later use.

Fresh Beef Stock

MAKES
1.75 LITRES/3 PINTS

about 1 kg/2 lb 4 oz bones from a cooked
    joint or raw chopped beef
2 onions, studded with 6 cloves, or sliced
    or chopped coarsely
2 carrots, sliced
1 leek, sliced
1–2 celery sticks, sliced
1 Bouquet Garni
about 2.25 litres/4 pints water

1 Use chopped marrow bones with
   a few strips of shin of beef, if
   possible. Put in a roasting tin and
   cook in a preheated oven,
   230°C/450°F/Gas Mark 8, for
   30–50 minutes, until browned.

2 Transfer to a large saucepan with
   the other ingredients. Bring
   to the boil and remove any scum
   from the surface with a large
   flat spoon.

3 Reduce the heat, cover and
   simmer gently for 3–4 hours.
   Strain the stock and leave to cool.
   Remove any fat from the surface
   and chill. If stored for more than
   24 hours the stock must be boiled
   every day, cooled quickly and
   chilled again.

4 The stock may be frozen for up to
   2 months; place in a large plastic
   bag and seal, leaving at least 2.5-
   cm/1-inch of headspace to allow
   for expansion.

Fresh Fish Stock

MAKES
1.75 LITRES/3 PINTS

1 kg/2 lb 4 oz white fish bones, heads
    and scraps
1 large onion, chopped
2 carrots, chopped
2 celery sticks, chopped
½ tsp black peppercorns
½ tsp grated lemon rind
few sprigs of fresh parsley
2 litres/3½ pints water
salt and pepper

1 Rinse the fish trimmings in cold
   water and place them in a large
   saucepan with the rest of
   the ingredients.

2 Bring to the boil and skim off
   any surface scum with a large
   flat spoon.

3 Reduce the heat and simmer,
   partially covered, for 30 minutes.
   Leave to cool.

4 Line a sieve with clean muslin
   and place over a large jug or bowl.
   Pour the stock through the sieve.
   Discard the solids. Cover the stock
   and store in the refrigerator for
   up to 3 days until required, or
   freeze in small batches.

How to Use This Book

Each recipe contains a wealth of useful information, including a breakdown of nutritional quantities, preparation and cooking times, and level of difficulty. All of this information is explained in detail below.

A full-colour photograph of the finished dish.

The ingredients for each recipe are listed in the order that they are used.

The nutritional information provided for each recipe is per serving or per portion. Optional ingredients, variations or serving suggestions have not been included in the calculations.

The method is clearly explained with step-by-step instructions that are easy to follow.

Cook's tips provide useful information regarding ingredients or cooking techniques.

The number of stars represents the difficulty of each recipe, ranging from very easy (1 star) to challenging (4 stars).

This amount of time represents the preparation of ingredients, including cooling, chilling and soaking times.

This represents the cooking time.

Soups

Chicken soup has an established reputation of being comforting and good for us and some cultures even regard it as a cure for all ills. It is certainly satisfying, full of flavour and easy to digest. For the best results, use a good home-made chicken stock, although when time is at a premium, a good-quality stock cube can be used instead. Every cuisine in the world has its own favourite version of chicken soup and in this section you'll find a selection of recipes from as far afield as Italy, Ireland, Scotland and China.

This light, refreshing soup with its tangy lemon flavour is perfect for a summer's day.

Lemon Chicken Soup

SERVES 4

55 g/2 oz butter
8 shallots, sliced thinly
2 carrots, sliced thinly
2 celery stalks, sliced thinly
250 g/9 oz skinless, boneless chicken breast, chopped finely
rind and juice of 3 lemons
1.25 litres/2 pints chicken stock
150 ml/5 fl oz double cream
salt and pepper

to garnish
sprigs of fresh parsley
lemon slices

1 Melt the butter in a large saucepan, add the vegetables and chicken and cook gently for 8 minutes.

2 Blanch the lemon rind in boiling water for 3 minutes. Add the lemon rind and lemon juice to the pan with the chicken stock and bring slowly to the boil.

3 Reduce the heat and simmer for about 50 minutes. Leave the soup to cool, then transfer to a food processor and blend until smooth.

4 Return the soup to the pan, reheat, season with salt and pepper to taste and add the double cream. Do not boil at this stage or the soup will curdle.

5 Transfer the soup to a warm tureen or individual bowls. Serve, garnished with parsley and lemon slices.

NUTRITION

Calories *560*; Sugars *4 g*; Protein *19 g*;
Carbohydrate *41 g*; Fat *31 g*; Saturates *19 g*

 easy
15 mins
1 hr 15 mins

 COOK'S TIP

For an alternative citrus flavour, use 4 oranges in place of the lemons. The recipe can also be adapted to make duck and orange soup.

Potatoes have been part of the Irish diet for centuries. This recipe is originally from the north of Ireland, in the beautiful area of Moira, County Down.

Irish Chicken Soup

1 Gently dry-fry the bacon and chicken in a large saucepan for 10 minutes.

2 Add the butter, potatoes and onions and cook for 15 minutes, stirring all the time.

3 Add the stock and milk, then bring to the boil. Reduce the heat and simmer for 45 minutes. Season with salt and pepper to taste.

4 Blend in the cream and simmer for 5 minutes. Stir in the parsley, then transfer the soup to a warm tureen or individual bowls and serve with soda bread.

SERVES 4

3 smoked, streaky, rindless bacon rashers, chopped
500 g/1 lb 2 oz skinless, boneless chicken, chopped
25 g/1 oz butter
3 potatoes, chopped
3 onions, chopped
600 ml/1 pint giblet or chicken stock
600 ml/1 pint milk
salt and pepper
150 ml/5 fl oz double cream
2 tbsp chopped fresh parsley
soda bread, to serve

NUTRITION
Calories 97; Sugars 2 g; Protein 7 g; Carbohydrate 4 g; Fat 2 g; Saturates 3 g

 moderate

 10 mins

 1 hr 20 mins

🍳 **COOK'S TIP**

Unlike most breads, soda bread is not made with yeast. Instead it uses bicarbonate of soda as the raising agent. It can be made with plain or wholemeal flour.

This satisfying and filling soup can be served as a main course. You can add rice and peppers to make it even more hearty, as well as colourful.

Chicken *and* Leek Soup

SERVES 6

25 g/1 oz butter
350 g/12 oz skinless, boneless chicken, cut into 2.5-cm/1-inch pieces
350 g/12 oz leeks, cut into 2.5-cm/1-inch pieces
1.25 litres/2 pints Fresh Chicken Stock (see p.14)
1 bouquet garni, fresh or dried
8 ready-to eat stoned prunes, halved
cooked rice and diced red pepper (optional)
salt and white pepper

1 Melt the butter in a large saucepan. Add the chicken and leeks and fry for 8 minutes, stirring occasionally.

2 Add the chicken stock and bouquet garni, and season with salt and pepper to taste.

3 Bring the soup to the boil, then reduce the heat and simmer over a gentle heat for 45 minutes.

4 Add the prunes with some cooked rice and red pepper, if using, and simmer for 20 minutes. Remove the bouquet garni and discard. Transfer the soup to a warm tureen or individual bowls and serve.

NUTRITION
Calories *183*; Sugars *4 g*; Protein *21 g*; Carbohydrate *4 g*; Fat *9 g*; Saturates *5 g*

 very easy

 5 mins

1 hr 15 mins

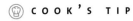 COOK'S TIP
If you have time, make the chicken stock yourself. Alternatively, you can buy good fresh stock from most supermarkets.

Quick to make, this hot and spicy soup is hearty and warming. If you like your food really fiery, add a chopped dried or fresh chilli with its seeds.

Thai-spiced Chicken Soup

1 Put the noodles in a shallow dish and soak in boiling water, according to the instructions on the packet, then drain well.

2 Heat the oil in a large saucepan or preheated wok. Add the chicken, and fry for 5 minutes, stirring until lightly browned. Add the white part of the spring onions, the garlic and ginger and fry for 2 minutes, stirring.

3 Add the stock, coconut milk, curry paste, peanut butter and soy sauce. Season with salt and pepper to taste, then bring to the boil. Reduce the heat and simmer for 8 minutes, stirring occasionally. Add the red pepper, peas and green spring onion tops and cook for 2 minutes.

4 Add the cooked noodles and heat through. Transfer the soup to individual bowls and serve with a spoon and fork.

SERVES 4

1 sheet of dried egg noodles from a 250 g/9 oz pack
1 tbsp oil
4 skinless, boneless chicken thighs, diced
1 bunch spring onions, green and white parts separated, sliced
2 garlic cloves, chopped
2-cm/³⁄₄-inch piece of fresh root ginger, chopped finely
900 ml/1½ pints chicken stock
200 ml/7 fl oz coconut milk
3 tsp Thai red curry paste
3 tbsp peanut butter
2 tbsp light soy sauce
1 small red pepper, deseeded and chopped
55 g/2 oz frozen peas
salt and pepper

NUTRITION
Calories *196*; Sugars *4 g*; Protein *16 g*; Carbohydrate *8 g*; Fat *11 g*; Saturates *2 g*

easy

10 mins

25 mins

(☺) **COOK'S TIP**

If preferred, Thai green curry paste can be used instead of red curry paste for a slightly less fiery flavour.

This satisfying soup makes a good lunch or supper dish, and you can use any vegetables that you have at hand. Children will love the tiny pasta shapes.

Chicken *and* Pasta Broth

SERVES 6

2 tbsp sunflower oil
350 g/12 oz skinless, boneless chicken breasts, diced
1 onion, diced
250 g/9 oz carrots, diced
250 g/9 oz cauliflower florets
900 ml/1½ pints chicken stock
2 tsp dried mixed herbs
125 g/4½ oz small pasta shapes
Parmesan cheese (optional)
salt and pepper
crusty bread, to serve

1 Heat the oil in a large saucepan and sauté the chicken and vegetables until they are lightly coloured.

2 Stir in the stock and herbs. Bring to the boil and add the pasta shapes. Return to the boil, then reduce the heat, cover and simmer for 10 minutes, stirring occasionally to prevent the pasta shapes sticking together.

3 Season with salt and pepper to taste. Transfer the soup to a warm tureen or individual bowls and sprinkle with Parmesan cheese, if using. Serve with fresh crusty bread.

NUTRITION

Calories *295*; Sugars *8 g*; Protein *25 g*; Carbohydrate *29 g*; Fat *10 g*; Saturates *2 g*

 easy

 10 mins

10 mins

20 mins

COOK'S TIP

You can use any small pasta shapes for this soup – try conchigliette, ditalini or even spaghetti broken into small pieces. To make a fun soup for children, you could add animal-shaped or alphabet pasta.

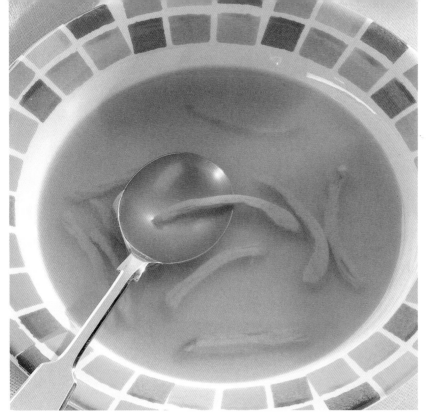

This is a very flavoursome soup, especially if you make it with real chicken stock. Egg shells and whites are used to give it a crystal clear appearance.

Chicken Consommé

1 Place the chicken stock and sherry in a large saucepan and heat gently for 5 minutes.

2 Add the egg whites and egg shells to the chicken stock and whisk until the mixture begins to boil.

3 Remove the pan from the heat and allow the mixture to rest for 10 minutes. Repeat this process 3 times. (This allows the egg white to trap the sediments in the chicken stock to clarify the soup.) Leave the consommé to cool for 5 minutes.

4 Carefully place a piece of fine muslin over a clean saucepan. Ladle the soup over the muslin and strain into the saucepan.

5 Repeat this process twice, then gently reheat the consommé. Season with salt and pepper to taste, then add the cooked chicken slices. Transfer the soup to a warm tureen or individual bowls.

SERVES **8 – 10**

1.75 litres/3 pints chicken stock
150 ml/5 fl oz medium sherry
4 egg whites, plus egg shells
115 g/4 oz cooked chicken, sliced thinly
salt and pepper

NUTRITION
Calories *96*; Sugars *1 g*; Protein *11 g*;
Carbohydrate *1 g*; Fat *1 g*; Saturates *0.4 g*

 challenging
 1 hr 15 mins
15 mins

🍳 COOK'S TIP

Consommé is usually garnished with freshly cooked pasta shapes, noodles, rice or lightly cooked vegetables. Alternatively, you could garnish it with omelette strips, drained first on kitchen paper.

This spicy soup was brought to the West by army and service personnel returning from India. It's perfect for a cold day.

Spicy Mulligatawny Soup

SERVES 4

55 g/2 oz butter
1 onion, sliced
1 garlic clove, crushed
500 g/1 lb 2 oz chicken meat, diced
55 g/2 oz smoked, rindless bacon, diced
1 small turnip, diced
2 carrots, diced
1 small cooking apple, diced
2 tbsp mild curry powder
1 tbsp curry paste
1 tbsp tomato purée
1 tbsp plain flour
1.25 litres/2 pints chicken stock
salt and pepper
150 ml/5 fl oz double cream
1 tsp chopped fresh coriander, to garnish
plain or fried rice, to serve

1 Melt the butter in a large saucepan and cook the onion, garlic, chicken and bacon for 5 minutes.

2 Add the turnip, carrots and apple and cook for a further 2 minutes.

3 Blend in the curry powder, curry paste and tomato purée and sprinkle over the plain flour.

4 Add the chicken stock and bring to the boil. Reduce the heat, cover and simmer over a gentle heat for about 1 hour.

5 Liquidize the soup in a blender or food processor. Reheat, season with salt and pepper to taste and gradually blend in the double cream. Transfer the soup to a warm tureen or individual soup bowls, garnished with coriander. Serve with small bowls of rice.

NUTRITION
Calories 502; Sugars 10 g; Protein 31 g;
Carbohydrate 17 g; Fat 35 g; Saturates 20 g

 easy

15 mins

1 hr 15 mins

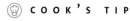 **COOK'S TIP**

This soup may be frozen for up to 1 month; if stored for any longer, the spices may cause it to taste musty.

A hearty soup that is so simple to make, yet is packed with flavour. You can use either whole green peas or green or yellow split peas.

Chicken *and* Split Pea Soup

1 Put the bacon, chicken and onion into a large saucepan with the butter and cook over a gentle heat for 8 minutes.

2 Add the soaked peas and the stock to the pan, then bring to the boil. Reduce the heat, season lightly with salt and pepper, cover and simmer for 2 hours.

3 Stir the double cream into the soup. Transfer the soup to a warm tureen or individual bowls, sprinkle with parsley and top with the cheesy croûtes.

S E R V E S 6

3 smoked, streaky, rindless bacon slices, chopped
900 g/2 lb chicken meat, chopped
1 large onion, chopped
15 g/½ oz butter
500 g/1 lb 2 oz ready-soaked peas
2.4 litres/4 pints chicken stock
150 ml/5 fl oz pint double cream
2 tbsp chopped fresh parsley
salt and pepper
cheesy croûtes, to serve

N U T R I T I O N
Calories *443*; Sugars *4* g; Protein *43* g;
Carbohydrate *21* g; Fat *21* g; Saturates *11 g*

★★★   moderate
   10 mins
   2 hrs 10 mins

🎩 **C O O K ' S   T I P**

Use 100 g/3½ oz chopped ham instead of the bacon, if preferred. If using dried peas, soak them for several hours or overnight in large bowl of cold water, then drain well before use.

Tarragon adds a delicate aniseed flavour to this tasty soup. If you can't find tarragon, use parsley for a fresh taste.

Chicken *and* Tarragon Soup

SERVES 4

55 g/2 oz unsalted butter
1 large onion, chopped
300 g/10½ oz cooked skinless chicken, shredded finely
600 ml/1 pint chicken stock
1 tbsp chopped fresh tarragon
150 ml/5 fl oz double cream
salt and pepper
fresh tarragon leaves, to garnish
deep-fried croûtons, to serve

1 Melt the butter in a large saucepan and fry the onion for 3 minutes.

2 Add the chicken to the pan with 300 ml/10 fl oz of the chicken stock.

3 Bring to the boil, then reduce the heat and simmer for 20 minutes. Leave to cool, then liquidize in a blender or food processor.

4 Add the remainder of the stock and season with salt and pepper to taste.

5 Add the chopped tarragon, then transfer the soup to a warm tureen or individual serving bowls and stir in the cream.

6 Garnish the soup with fresh tarragon and serve with deep-fried croûtons.

NUTRITION
Calories *434*; Sugars *4 g*; Protein *22 g*;
Carbohydrate *6 g*; Fat *36 g*; Saturates *21 g*

 easy

10 mins

30 mins

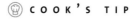 **COOK'S TIP**

To make garlic croûtons, crush 3–4 garlic cloves in a pestle and mortar and add to the oil before frying.

Use the vegetables and chicken to make little patties. Simply mash with a little butter, shape them into round cakes and fry until golden brown.

Chicken Soup *with* Dumplings

1 Coat the chicken pieces with seasoned flour.

2 Melt the butter in a saucepan and fry the chicken pieces until they are lightly browned.

3 Add the oil to the pan and brown the vegetables. Add the sherry and herbs.

4 Cook for 10 minutes, then add the stock and bring to the boil. Season with salt and pepper to taste. Reduce the heat and simmer for 3 hours, then strain into a clean saucepan and leave to cool.

5 To make the dumplings, mix together all the dry ingredients in a large clean bowl. Add the egg, season, and blend thoroughly, then add enough milk to make a moist dough. Shape into small balls and roll them in a little flour.

6 Cook the dumplings in boiling salted water for 10 minutes.

7 Remove the dumplings carefully with a slotted spoon and add them to the soup and cook for a further 12 minutes. Transfer the soup to a warm tureen or individual soup bowls. Garnish with sprigs of coriander and serve with crusty bread.

S E R V E S 6

900 g/2 lb skinless chicken meat, sliced
55 g/2 oz plain flour
125 g/4½ oz butter
3 tbsp sunflower oil
1 large carrot, chopped
1 stick celery, chopped
1 onion, chopped
1 small turnip, chopped
120 ml/4 fl oz sherry
1 tsp thyme
1 bay leaf
1.75 litres/3 pints chicken stock
salt and pepper
sprigs of fresh coriander, to garnish
crusty bread, to serve

dumplings
55 g/2 oz self-raising flour
55 g/2 oz fresh breadcrumbs
2 tbsp shredded suet
2 tbsp chopped fresh coriander
2 tbsp finely grated lemon rind
1 egg

N U T R I T I O N
Calories *578*; Sugars *6 g*; Protein *39 g*;
Carbohydrate *30 g*; Fat *32 g*; Saturates *16 g*

 moderate

 25 mins

3 hrs 40 mins

CHICKEN

This soup is made with traditional Scottish ingredients. It should be left for at least a day before being reheated, then served with oat cakes or crusty bread.

Scottish Chicken *and* Barley Broth

SERVES 4

55 g/2 oz pre-soaked dried split peas
900 g/2 lb skinless chicken, diced
1.25 litres/2 pints chicken stock
600 ml/1 pint water
55 g/2 oz barley, rinsed
1 large carrot, diced
1 small turnip, diced
1 large leek, sliced thinly
1 red onion, chopped finely
salt and white pepper

1 Put the split peas and chicken into a large saucepan. Add the stock and water, then bring slowly to the boil. Skim the stock as it boils using a slotted spoon.

2 When any scum has been removed from the surface, add the barley and season with salt. Reduce the heat and simmer for 35 minutes.

3 Add the remaining ingredients and simmer for a further 2 hours. Season with salt and white pepper to taste.

4 Skim the surface of the soup again and leave the broth to stand for at least 24 hours. Reheat, adjust the seasoning and serve.

NUTRITION
Calories *357*; Sugars *5 g*; Protein *53 g*;
Carbohydrate *19 g*; Fat *8 g*; Saturates *2 g*

⊛⊛   easy
◔   24 hrs 15 mins
◕   2 hrs 45 mins

 COOK'S TIP

Use either wholegrain barley or pearl barley. Only the outer husk is removed from the wholegrain variety and it has a nutty flavour and chewy texture when cooked.

For a tangy flavour, lemons can be used instead of oranges and the recipe can be adapted to make a duck and orange soup.

Orange, Chicken *and* Carrot Soup

1 Melt the butter in a large saucepan. Add the shallots, carrot, celery and chicken and cook gently for 8 minutes, stirring occasionally.

2 Blanch the orange rind in boiling water for about 3 minutes.

3 Add the orange rind and orange juice to the pan with the chicken stock, then bring to the boil.

4 Reduce the heat and simmer for 50 minutes. Leave the soup to cool, then liquidize in a blender or food processor until smooth.

5 Return the soup to the saucepan, reheat, season with salt and pepper to taste and add the cream. Do not allow the soup to boil at this stage or the soup will curdle.

6 Transfer the soup to a warm tureen or individual bowls. Garnish with sprigs of parsley and orange slices, and serve with soda bread.

S E R V E S 4

55 g/2 oz butter
8 shallots, sliced thinly
2 carrots, sliced thinly
2 celery sticks, sliced thinly
250 g/8 oz skinless chicken breast, finely chopped
thinly pared rind and juice of 3 oranges
1.25 litres/2 pints chicken stock
150 ml/5 fl oz double cream
salt and white pepper
soda bread, to serve

to garnish
sprigs of fresh parsley
orange slices

N U T R I T I O N
Calories *420*; Sugars *16 g*; Protein *18 g*; Carbohydrate *16 g*; Fat *32 g*; Saturates *20 g*

moderate

15 mins

1 hr 10 mins

🔘 **C O O K ' S T I P**

Use 2 small lemons in place of the oranges. Look for organic or unwaxed oranges or lemons when using the rind.

Guinea fowl has a similar texture to chicken. Although it has a milder flavour than other game, it has a slightly stronger flavour than chicken.

Chicken *and* Pasta Soup

SERVES 6

500 g/1 lb 2 oz skinless chicken meat, chopped
500 g/1 lb 2 oz skinless guinea fowl meat, chopped
600 ml/1 pint chicken stock
1 small onion
6 peppercorns
1 tsp cloves
pinch of mace
150 ml/5 fl oz double cream
15 g/½ oz butter
2 tsp plain flour
125 g/4½ oz quick-cook spaghetti, broken into short lengths and cooked
2 tbsp chopped fresh parsley, to garnish

1 Put the chicken and guinea fowl meat into a large saucepan then add the chicken stock.

2 Bring to the boil and add the onion, peppercorns, cloves and mace. Reduce the heat and simmer the soup very gently for about 2 hours, until the stock has reduced by one-third.

3 Strain the soup and skim off any fat.

4 Return the soup and meat to a clean pan. Add the double cream and bring slowly to the boil.

5 To make a roux, melt the butter and stir in the flour until it has a paste-like consistency. Add to the soup, stirring until slightly thickened.

6 Just before serving, add the cooked spaghetti.

7 Transfer the soup to a warm tureen or individual serving bowls, garnish with parsley and serve.

NUTRITION
Calories *418*; Sugars *2 g*; Protein *40 g*;
Carbohydrate *18 g*; Fat *21 g*; Saturates *11 g*

 easy

 20 mins

 2 hrs 15 mins

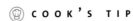 COOK'S TIP

Instead of spaghetti, use small pasta shapes such as zite or macaroni.

This soup is excellent made with fresh tomatoes, but you can use canned tomatoes, although the flavour isn't quite as good.

Fresh Tomato *and* Chicken Soup

1 Melt the butter in a large saucepan and fry the onion and chicken for 5 minutes.

2 Add 300 ml/10 fl oz of the chicken stock to the pan, with the tomatoes and bicarbonate of soda, then bring the soup to the boil. Reduce the heat and simmer for 20 minutes.

3 Leave the soup to cool, then blend in a blender or food processor.

4 Add the remaining chicken stock, season with salt and pepper to taste, then add the sugar. Bring almost to the boil, then transfer the soup to a warm tureen or individual bowls. Add a swirl of double cream, garnish with fresh basil and serve.

SERVES 4

55 g/2 oz unsalted butter
1 large onion, chopped
500 g/1 lb 2 oz skinless chicken meat, shredded very finely
600 ml/1 pint chicken stock
6 tomatoes, chopped finely
pinch of bicarbonate of soda
1 tbsp caster sugar
150 ml/5 fl oz double cream
salt and pepper
sprigs of fresh basil leaves, to garnish

NUTRITION
Calories *481*; Sugars *14 g*; Protein *30 g*; Carbohydrate *15 g*; Fat *34 g*; Saturates *20 g*

easy

15 mins

35 mins

🍳 **COOK'S TIP**

For an Italian-style soup, add 1 tablespoon of chopped fresh basil with the stock in step 2. Alternatively, add ½ teaspoon curry powder or chilli powder to make a spicier version of this soup.

This Chinese-style soup is delicious as a starter to an Oriental meal or as a light meal served on its own.

Chicken Wonton Soup

SERVES 6

1.5 litres/2½ pints chicken stock
1 tbsp light soy sauce
1 spring onion, shredded
1 small carrot, cut into very thin slices

wontons

350 g/12 oz minced chicken
1 tbsp soy sauce
1 tsp grated fresh root ginger
1 garlic clove, crushed
2 tsp sherry
2 spring onions, chopped
1 tsp sesame oil
1 egg white
½ tsp cornflour
½ tsp sugar
about 35 wonton wrappers

1 Combine all the ingredients for the wontons, except the wrappers, and mix well. Place a small spoonful of the filling in the centre of each wonton wrapper.

2 Dampen the edges and gather up the wonton wrapper to form a pouch enclosing the filling.

3 Cook the filled wontons in boiling water for 1 minute, or until they float to the top. Remove with a slotted spoon.

4 Bring the chicken stock to the boil. Add the soy sauce, spring onion, carrot and wontons to the soup. Reduce the heat and simmer gently for 2 minutes. Transfer the soup to a warm tureen or individual bowls and serve.

NUTRITION

Calories *401*; Sugars *6 g*; Protein *31 g*; Carbohydrate *17 g*; Fat *24 g*; Saturates *13 g*

easy

20 mins

15 mins

🍳 COOK'S TIP

Look for wonton wrappers in Chinese or Oriental supermarkets. Fresh wrappers can be found in the chilled compartment and they can be frozen if wished. Wrap in clingfilm before freezing.

A traditional Scottish soup in which a whole chicken is cooked with the vegetables to add a rich flavour to the stock.

Cock-a-leekie Soup

1 Put the chicken, giblets, if using, stock and onion in a large saucepan. Bring to the boil and skim off any scum that rises to the surface.

2 Add the leeks, allspice and bouquet garni to the pan, season with salt and pepper to taste. Reduce the heat, cover and simmer gently for about 1½ hours, until the chicken meat is beginning to fall off the bones.

3 Remove the chicken and bouquet garni from the pan and skim any fat from the surface of the soup.

4 Chop some of the chicken flesh and return to the pan. Add the prunes and bring back to the boil. Reduce the heat and simmer, uncovered, for about 20 minutes. Taste and adjust the seasoning, if necessary, and serve with warm crusty bread.

SERVES 4 – 6

1–1.5 kg/2lb 4 oz–3 lb 5 oz oven-ready chicken, plus giblets, if available
1.75–2 litres/3–3½ pints Fresh Chicken Stock (see p.14)
1 onion, sliced
4 leeks, sliced thinly
pinch of ground allspice or ground coriander
1 bouquet garni
12 ready-to-eat prunes, halved and stoned
salt and pepper
warm crusty bread, to serve

NUTRITION
Calories *45*; Sugars *4 g*; Protein *5 g*; Carbohydrate *5 g*; Fat *1 g*; Saturates *0.2 g*

★★   easy

○   30 mins

●   2 hrs

🍳 COOK'S TIP

You can replace the chicken stock with 3 chicken stock cubes, dissolved in the same amount of water, if preferred.

Tender cooked chicken strips and baby corn cobs are the main flavours in this delicious clear soup, with just a hint of ginger.

Curried Chicken Soup

SERVES 4

175 g/6 oz canned sweetcorn, drained
850 ml/1½ pints chicken stock
350 g/12 oz cooked skinless chicken meat,
    cut into strips
16 baby corn cobs
1 tsp Chinese curry powder
1-cm/½-inch piece of fresh root ginger,
    grated
3 tbsp light soy sauce
2 tbsp chopped fresh chives

1 Place the sweetcorn in a food processor, with 150 ml/5 fl oz pint of the chicken stock and process until the mixture forms a smooth purée.

2 Pass the sweetcorn purée through a fine sieve, pressing with the back of a spoon to remove any husks.

3 Pour the remaining chicken stock into a large saucepan and add the chicken. Stir in the sweetcorn purée to combine.

4 Add the baby corn cobs and bring the soup to the boil. Boil over a medium heat for 10 minutes.

5 Add the Chinese curry powder, ginger and light soy sauce and stir well to combine. Reduce the heat and simmer for a further 10–15 minutes.

6 Stir in the chopped chives. Transfer the soup to a warm tureen or individual bowls and serve immediately.

NUTRITION
Calories *206*; Sugars *5 g*; Protein *29 g*;
Carbohydrate *13 g*; Fat *5 g*; Saturates *1 g*

easy

10 mins

30 mins

🍴 **COOK'S TIP**

Prepare the soup up to 24 hours in advance, without adding the chicken. Cool, cover and store in the refrigerator. Add the chicken and heat the soup through thoroughly before serving.

How delicious a simple, fresh soup can be. Chicken wings are good to use for making the stock, as the meat is very sweet and doesn't dry out.

Chicken Soup *with* Stars

1 Put the chicken in a large flameproof casserole with the water, celery, carrot, onion, leek, garlic, peppercorns, allspice, herbs and half a teaspoon of salt. Bring just to the boil and skim off the scum that rises to the surface. Reduce the heat, partially cover, and simmer for 2 hours.

2 Remove the chicken from the stock and set aside to cool. Continue to simmer the stock, uncovered, for about 30 minutes. When the chicken is cool enough to handle, remove the meat from the bones and, if necessary, cut into bite-sized pieces.

3 Strain the stock and remove as much fat as possible. Discard the vegetables and flavourings. (There should be about 1.7 litres/3 pints chicken stock.)

4 Bring the stock to the boil in a clean pan. Add the pasta and reduce the heat so that the stock boils very gently. Cook for about 10 minutes, or until the pasta is tender, but still firm to the bite.

5 Stir in the chicken meat. Adjust the seasoning, if necessary. Transfer the soup to a warm tureen or individual soup bowls and serve sprinkled with parsley.

SERVES **4**

85 g/3 oz small pasta stars, or other very small shapes
chopped fresh parsley, to garnish

chicken stock

1.25 kg/2 lb 12 oz chicken pieces, such as wings or legs
2.5 litres/4½ pints water
1 celery stick, sliced
1 large carrot, sliced
1 onion, sliced
1 leek, sliced
2 garlic cloves, crushed
8 peppercorns
4 allspice berries
3–4 parsley stems
2–3 sprigs of fresh thyme
1 bay leaf
salt and pepper
chopped fresh parsely, to garnish

NUTRITION
Calories 119; Sugars 2 g; Protein 14 g; Carbohydrate 13 g; Fat 2 g; Saturates 0 g

 moderate

 30 mins

2 hrs 45 mins

Snacks *and* Starters

Since chicken is so versatile and quick to cook, it is perfect
for innovative and appetizing snacks. Its unassertive
flavour means that it can be enlivened by exotic fruits
and spices and Oriental ingredients, such as mirin,
sesame oil and fresh ginger. There are fritters, salads and
drumsticks that are stuffed and baked, or served with
delicious fruity salsas. As cooked chicken travels well and
is easy to eat, many of the recipes are ideal to take
on picnics or to pack into a lunchbox.

Use the breasts from a roasted chicken for this delicious, healthy snack. Served with a mixed salad, it is an ideal light meal for a summer's day.

Jacket Potatoes *with* Chicken

SERVES 4

4 large baking potatoes, pricked
250 g/9 oz cooked skinless, boneless chicken breasts, diced
4 spring onions, sliced thickly
250 g/9 oz low-fat soft cheese
pepper
green salad or mixed salad, to serve

1 Bake the potatoes in a preheated oven, 200°C/400°F/Gas Mark 6, for about 60 minutes, until tender, or cook in a microwave on High power for 12–15 minutes.

2 Mix the chicken and spring onions with the low-fat soft cheese.

3 Cut a cross through the top of each potato and squeeze slightly apart. Spoon the chicken filling into the potatoes and season with pepper. Serve immediately with a green or mixed salad.

NUTRITION

Calories *417*; Sugars *4 g*; Protein *28 g*; Carbohydrate *57 g*; Fat *10 g*; Saturates *5 g*

 very easy
10 mins
 1 hr

🍳 COOK'S TIP

Low-fat ricotta cheese or low-fat fromage frais can be used as alternatives to soft cheese in this recipe.

These tasty sandwiches are good as a snack on their own or they can be served as part of a picnic spread.

Open Chicken Sandwiches

1 Reserve the yolk and the white from 1 egg separately.

2 In a large bowl, mix the remaining egg with the softened butter, English mustard and anchovy essence and season with pepper to taste.

3 Mix in the Cheddar and chicken and spread the mixture on the bread.

4 Make alternate rows of the reserved egg yolk and white on top of the chicken mixture. Arrange the tomato and cucumber slices on top of the egg and serve.

SERVES **6**

3 hard-boiled eggs, the yolk sieved and the white chopped
25 g/1 oz butter, softened
2 tbsp English mustard
1 tsp anchovy essence
250 g/9 oz Cheddar cheese, grated
3 cooked skinless chicken breasts, chopped finely
6 thick slices of bread or a large French stick cut lengthways, then cut into 6 pieces and buttered
12 slices each of tomato and cucumber
pepper

NUTRITION
Calories 510; Sugars 3 g; Protein 34 g; Carbohydrate 8 g; Fat 22 g; Saturates 18 g

 very easy
15 mins
0 mins

🍳 **COOK'S TIP**

If you prefer a milder flavour, use a mild mustard. Add mayonnaise, if liked, and garnish with watercress.

All the sunshine colours and flavours of the Mediterranean are combined in this easy dish.

Chicken Peperonata

SERVES 4

8 skinless chicken thighs
2 tbsp wholemeal flour
2 tbsp olive oil
1 small onion, sliced thinly
1 garlic clove, crushed
1 each large red, yellow and green peppers,
   deseeded and sliced thinly
400 g/14 oz canned chopped tomatoes
1 tbsp chopped fresh oregano, plus extra
   to garnish
salt and pepper
crusty wholemeal bread, to serve

1 Toss the chicken thighs in the flour.

2 Heat the oil in a large, heavy-based frying pan and fry the chicken quickly until sealed and lightly browned, then remove from the pan. Add the onion to the pan and gently cook for 5 minutes, until softened. Add the garlic, peppers, tomatoes and oregano, then bring to the boil, stirring.

3 Arrange the chicken over the vegetables, and season with salt and pepper to taste. Reduce the heat, cover and simmer for 20–25 minutes, or until the chicken is completely cooked and tender.

4 Adjust the seasoning, if necessary, garnish with extra oregano and serve with crusty wholemeal bread.

NUTRITION
Calories 328; Sugars 7 g; Protein 35 g;
Carbohydrate 13 g; Fat 15 g; Saturates 4 g

easy

15 mins

40 mins

🍳 **COOK'S TIP**

For extra flavour, halve and deseed the peppers and cook under a preheated grill until the skins char. Leave to cool, then remove the skins. Slice the peppers thinly and use in the recipe.

These fritters are delicious served with a mixed salad, a fresh vegetable salsa or a chilli sauce dip.

Chicken *and* Herb Fritters

1 In a large bowl, blend the potatoes, chicken, ham, herbs and 1 of the eggs, and season with salt and pepper to taste.

2 Shape the mixture into small balls or flat pancakes.

3 Add a little milk to the second egg.

4 Place the breadcrumbs on a plate. Dip the balls in the egg and milk mixture, then roll in the breadcrumbs, to coat them completely.

5 Heat the oil in a large, heavy-based frying pan and cook the fritters until they are golden brown. Garnish with sprigs of fresh parsley and serve with a mixed salad.

MAKES 8

500 g/1 lb 2 oz mashed potato, with butter added
250 g/9 oz cooked skinless chicken, chopped
125 g/4½ oz cooked ham, chopped finely
1 tbsp fresh mixed herbs
2 eggs, lightly beaten
salt and pepper
milk
125 g/4½ oz fresh wholemeal breadcrumbs
oil for shallow-frying
sprigs of fresh parsley, to garnish
mixed salad, to serve

NUTRITION
Calories 333; Sugars 1 g; Protein 16 g; Carbohydrate 17 g; Fat 23 g; Saturates 5 g

easy

25 mins

20 mins

 COOK'S TIP

Serve the fritters with a tomato sauce: heat 200 ml/7 fl oz passata and 4 tablespoons dry white wine. Season, remove from the heat and add 4 tablespoons natural yogurt. Reheat and add chilli powder to taste.

A low-fat chicken recipe with a refreshingly light, mustard-spiced sauce, which is ideal for a healthy lunchbox or a light meal with salad.

Baked Chicken *with* Rosemary

SERVES 4

25 g/1 oz rolled oats
1 tbsp chopped fresh rosemary
4 skinless chicken quarters
1 egg white
150 g/5½ oz natural low-fat fromage frais
2 tsp wholegrain mustard
salt and pepper
grated carrot salad, to serve

1 Mix together the rolled oats and rosemary, and season with salt and pepper to taste.

2 Brush each piece of chicken with egg white, then coat in the oat mixture. Place on a baking sheet and bake in a preheated oven, 200°C/400°F/Gas Mark 6, for about 40 minutes, or until the chicken juices run clear when pierced in the thickest part with a skewer.

3 In a bowl, mix together the fromage frais and wholegrain mustard, season, then serve with the hot or cold chicken and the carrot salad.

NUTRITION

Calories *120*; Sugars *3 g*; Protein *15 g*; Carbohydrate *8 g*; Fat *3 g*; Saturates *1 g*

  very easy

10 mins

40 mins

 COOK'S TIP

Add 1 tablespoon sesame or sunflower seeds to the oat mixture for an even crunchier texture. Experiment with different herbs, instead of the rosemary.

This attractive cold platter makes a delicious addition to a buffet party or a spectacular starter for a special meal.

Chicken *and* Herring Platter

1 Spread out the lettuce leaves on a large oval platter.

2 Arrange the chicken in 3 sections on the platter.

3 Place the rollmops, eggs and different meats in lines or sections over the remainder of the platter.

4 Use the mangetout, grapes, olives, shallots, almonds and sultanas to fill in the spaces between the sections.

5 Grate the rind from the oranges and sprinkle over the whole platter. Peel and slice the oranges and add to the platter with the mint sprig. Season with salt and pepper to taste. Sprinkle with the herring marinade and serve with crusty bread.

SERVES 4

1 large lettuce, separated into leaves
4 cooked chicken breasts, thinly sliced
8 rollmop herrings and their marinade
6 hard-boiled eggs, quartered
125 g/4½ oz cooked ham, sliced
125 g/4½ oz roast beef, sliced
125 g/4½ oz roast lamb, sliced
150 g/5½ oz cooked mangetout
125 g/4½ oz seedless black grapes,
20 stuffed olives, sliced
12 shallots, boiled
55 g/2 oz flaked almonds
55 g/2 oz sultanas
2 oranges
sprig of fresh mint
salt and pepper
fresh crusty bread, to serve

NUTRITION
Calories *740*; Sugars *62 g*; Protein *88 g*;
Carbohydrate *65 g*; Fat *34 g*; Saturates *9 g*

 moderate
 25 mins
0 mins

COOK'S TIP

The platter can be served with cold, cooked vegetable, such as French beans, baby sweetcorn and cooked beetroot, if liked.

Perfect for a picnic or packed lunch, this Mediterranean-style sandwich can be prepared in advance.

Mediterranean Pan Bagna

SERVES 6

1 garlic clove, halved
1 large French stick, cut lengthways
125 ml/4 fl oz olive oil
55 g/2 oz cold roast chicken, sliced thinly
2 large tomatoes, sliced
20 g/³⁄₄ oz canned anchovy fillets, drained
8 large, stoned black olives, chopped
pepper

1 Rub the garlic over the cut side of the bread and sprinkle with the olive oil.

2 Arrange the chicken on top of the bread. Arrange the tomatoes and anchovies on top of the chicken.

3 Scatter with the black olives and season with plenty of pepper. Sandwich the loaf back together and wrap tightly in foil until required. Cut into slices to serve.

NUTRITION
Calories *366*; Sugars *2 g*; Protein *20 g*;
Carbohydrate *20 g*; Fat *23 g*; Saturates *4 g*

 very easy
 10 mins
 0 mins

🧑‍🍳 **COOK'S TIP**

Arrange a few fresh basil leaves in between the tomato slices to add a warm, aromatic flavour. Use a good-quality olive oil in this recipe for extra flavour.

This classic salad is good as a starter or as part of a buffet. Mango chutney makes a tasty addition.

Coronation Chicken

1 Heat the oil in a large, heavy-based frying pan. Add the chicken, bacon, shallots, garlic and curry powder. Cook slowly, stirring, for about 15 minutes.

2 Spoon the mixture into a clean mixing bowl. Leave to cool completely, then season with pepper to taste.

3 Blend the mayonnaise with a little honey to taste, then add the chopped fresh parsley. Toss the chicken in the mayonnaise mixture.

4 Place the chicken in a serving dish, garnish with the grapes and serve with cold saffron rice.

SERVES 6

4 tbsp olive oil
900 g/2 lb skinless chicken, diced
125 g/4½ oz rindless, smoked bacon, diced
12 shallots
2 garlic cloves, crushed
1 tbsp mild curry powder
pepper
300 ml/10 fl oz mayonnaise
1 tbsp clear honey
1 tbsp chopped fresh parsley
85 g/3 oz seedless white grapes, quartered, to garnish
cold saffron rice, to serve

NUTRITION
Calories 660; Sugars 5 g; Protein 40 g; Carbohydrate 7 g; Fat 53 g; Saturates 9 g

 COOK'S TIP

You can use this recipe to fill a jacket potato or as a sandwich filling, but cut the chicken into smaller pieces.

very easy

10 mins

15 mins

A food processor makes light work of this recipe, but you can pound it by hand for a coarser mixture.

Chicken Pots *with* Port

SERVES 6

350 g/12 oz smoked chicken, chopped
pinch each of grated nutmeg and mace
125 g/4½ oz butter, softened
2 tbsp port
2 tbsp double cream
250 g/9 oz butter, for clarifying (see Cook's Tip)
salt and pepper
sprigs of fresh parsley, to garnish
sliced brown bread, to serve

1 Place the smoked chicken in a large bowl with the remaining ingredients, and season with salt and pepper to taste.

2 Pound until the mixture is very smooth or blend in a food processor.

3 Transfer the mixture to individual earthenware pots or one large pot.

4 Cover each pot with buttered baking paper and weigh down with cans or weights. Chill in the refrigerator for 4 hours.

5 Remove the paper and cover with clarified butter (see Cook's Tip).

6 Garnish each pot with a sprig of parsley and serve with slices of brown bread.

NUTRITION

Calories *345*; Sugars *1 g*; Protein *18 g*;
Carbohydrate *1 g*; Fat *29 g*; Saturates *19 g*

 easy

 4 hrs 20 mins

0 mins

🍴 **COOK'S TIP**

To make clarified butter: melt 250 g/9 oz of butter in a saucepan, skimming off the foam as the butter heats. When melted, remove from the heat and leave to stand for 4 minutes. Strain through muslin and leave to cool a little.

Ideal for informal parties, these tasty chicken drumsticks can be prepared a day in advance. Instead of baking the chicken drumsticks, you could cook them on the barbecue.

Cheesy Garlic Drummers

1 Melt the butter in a saucepan. Add the garlic and fry gently, stirring, for 1 minute without browning.

2 Remove the pan from the heat and stir in the parsley, the cheeses, fresh breadcrumbs and season with salt and pepper to taste.

3 Carefully loosen the skin around the chicken drumsticks.

4 Using a teaspoon, push about 1 tablespoon of the stuffing under the skin of each drumstick. Arrange the drumsticks in a large baking tin.

5 Bake in a preheated oven, 190°C/375°F/Gas Mark 5, for about 45 minutes. Garnish with lemon slices and serve hot or cold with mixed salad leaves.

SERVES 6

15 g/½ oz butter
1 garlic clove, crushed
3 tbsp chopped fresh parsley
125 g/4½ oz ricotta cheese
4 tbsp grated Parmesan cheese
3 tbsp fresh breadcrumbs
12 chicken drumsticks
salt and pepper
lemon slices, to garnish
mixed salad leaves, to serve

NUTRITION
Calories *241*; Sugars *0 g*; Protein *28 g*; Carbohydrate *4 g*; Fat *13 g*; Saturates *05 g*

moderate

25 mins

50 mins

🧑‍🍳 COOK'S TIP

Freshly grated Parmesan has more flavour than ready-packed grated Parmesan. Grate only as much as you need and wrap the rest in foil – it will keep for several months in the refrigerator.

A tasty dish that can be
served alone as a snack or
to accompany a light soup.

Cheese *and* Chicken Toasts

SERVES 4

250 g/9 oz Wensleydale cheese, grated
250 g/9 oz cooked chicken, shredded
25g/1 oz butter
1 tbsp Worcestershire sauce
1 tsp dry English mustard
2 tsp plain flour
4 tbsp mild beer
4 slices of bread
salt and pepper
1 tbsp chopped fresh parsley, to garnish
cherry tomatoes, to serve

1 Place the Wensleydale cheese, chicken, butter, Worcestershire sauce, mustard, plain flour and beer in a small saucepan. Mix all the ingredients together then season with salt and pepper to taste.

2 Gently bring the mixture to the boil, then remove from the heat.

3 Using a wooden spoon, beat the mixture until it becomes creamy in texture. Leave the mixture to cool.

4 Once the chicken mixture has cooled, toast the bread on both sides and spread with the chicken mixture.

5 Place under a hot grill and cook until bubbling and golden brown.

6 Garnish with a little chopped parsley and serve with cherry tomatoes.

NUTRITION
Calories *495*; Sugars *2 g*; Protein *35 g*;
Carbohydrate *21 g*; Fat *30 g*; Saturates *2 g*

easy

10 mins

10 mins

 COOK'S TIP

This is a variation of Welsh rarebit, which does not traditionally contain chicken. Welsh rarebit topped with a poached egg is called buck rarebit.

This colourful and healthy dish is a variation of a classic salad. Served with crusty brown rolls, it is an ideal light meal for a summer's day.

Waldorf Summer Chicken Salad

1 Place the apples in a bowl with the lemon juice and 1 tablespoon of the mayonnaise. Set aside for 40 minutes.

2 Add the celery, shallots, garlic and walnuts to the apple and mix together.

3 Stir in the remaining mayonnaise and blend thoroughly.

4 Add the cooked chicken to the bowl and mix well.

5 Line a glass salad bowl or serving dish with the lettuce leaves. Pile the chicken salad into the centre, sprinkle with pepper and garnish with the apple slices.

SERVES 4

500 g/1 lb 2 oz red apples, cored and diced
3 tbsp fresh lemon juice
150 ml/5 fl oz light mayonnaise
1 head of celery, sliced thinly
4 shallots, sliced thinly
1 garlic clove, crushed
85 g/3 oz walnuts, chopped
500 g/1 lb 2 oz cooked chicken, cubed
1 Cos lettuce, leaves separated
pepper
sliced apple, to garnish

NUTRITION
Calories *471*; Sugars *19 g*; Protein *38 g*; Carbohydrate *20 g*; Fat *27 g*; Saturates *4 g*

easy
50 mins
0 mins

COOK'S TIP

Use spring onions instead of the shallots for a milder flavour. Trim the spring onions and slice finely.

For this simple, refreshing summer salad you can use leftover roast chicken, or ready-roasted chicken. Add the dressing just before serving, or the spinach will lose its crispness.

Chicken *and* Spinach Salad

SERVES 4

3 celery sticks, sliced thinly
½ cucumber, sliced thinly
2 spring onions, sliced thinly
250 g/9 oz young spinach leaves
3 tbsp chopped fresh parsley
350g/12 oz boneless, roast chicken, sliced thinly

dressing

2.5-cm/1-inch piece of fresh root ginger, grated finely
3 tbsp olive oil
1 tbsp white wine vinegar
1 tbsp clear honey
½ tsp ground cinnamon
salt and pepper
smoked almonds, to garnish (optional)

1 Toss the celery, cucumber and spring onions in a large bowl with the spinach leaves and parsley.

2 Transfer the salad to serving plates and arrange the chicken on top.

3 In a screw-topped jar, combine all the dressing ingredients and shake well to mix. Season with salt and pepper to taste, then pour the dressing over the salad. Garnish with a few smoked almonds, if using.

NUTRITION
Calories *225*; Sugars *4 g*; Protein *25 g*; Carbohydrate *4 g*; Fat *12 g*; Saturates *2 g*

 very easy
 10 mins
0 mins

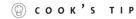 **COOK'S TIP**

Fresh young spinach leaves go particularly well with fruit – try adding a few fresh raspberries or nectarine slices to make a refreshing salad.

The sweetness of the pears complements perfectly the sharp taste of the blue cheese in this delicious warm salad.

Warm Chicken *and* Rice Salad

1 Place the olive oil, shallots, garlic, tarragon and mustard in a deep bowl. Season with salt and pepper to taste and mix well.

2 Place the chicken in the marinade and turn to coat completely, cover with clingfilm and chill in the refrigerator for about 4 hours.

3 Drain the chicken, reserving the marinade. Quickly fry the chicken in a large, heavy-based frying pan for 4 minutes on both sides. Transfer the chicken to a warm serving dish.

4 Add the marinade to the pan, bring to the boil and sprinkle with the flour. Reduce the heat, add the chicken stock, apple and walnuts and simmer for 5 minutes. Return the chicken to the sauce, add the double cream and cook for 2 minutes.

5 Mix the salad ingredients together, place a little on each plate and top with a chicken breast and a spoonful of the sauce.

SERVES 6

50 ml/2 fl oz olive oil
6 shallots, sliced
1 garlic clove, crushed
2 tbsp chopped fresh tarragon
1 tbsp English mustard
6 skinless, boneless chicken breasts
1 tbsp flour
150 ml/5 fl oz chicken stock
1 apple, cored and diced finely
1 tbsp chopped walnuts
2 tbsp double cream
salt and pepper

salad
250 g/9 oz cooked rice
2 large pears, cored and diced
150 g/5½ oz blue cheese, diced
1 red pepper, deseeded and diced
1 tbsp chopped fresh coriander
1 tbsp sesame oil

NUTRITION
Calories *605*; Sugars *13 g*; Protein *41 g*; Carbohydrate *52 g*; Fat *27 g*; Saturates *10 g*

 easy

 4 hrs 15 mins

20 mins

This colourful, simple dish will tempt the appetites of the whole family – children will enjoy the fun shapes of the multi-coloured peppers.

Harlequin Chicken

SERVES 4

1 tbsp sunflower oil
10 skinless, boneless chicken thighs, cut into bite-sized pieces
1 onion, sliced thinly
1 each red, green and yellow peppers, deseeded and cut into diamond shapes
400 g/14 oz canned chopped tomatoes
2 tbsp chopped fresh parsley
pepper

to serve
wholemeal bread
green salad

1 Heat the oil in a heavy-based frying pan. Add the chicken and onion and fry quickly until golden.

2 Add the red, green and yellow peppers and cook for 2–3 minutes, then stir in the tomatoes and parsley, and season with pepper to taste.

3 Cover tightly and simmer for about 15 minutes, until the chicken and vegetables are tender. Serve hot with wholemeal bread and a green salad.

NUTRITION
Calories *183*; Sugars *8 g*; Protein *24 g*; Carbohydrate *8 g*; Fat *6 g*; Saturates *1 g*

★ very easy
🕐 15 mins
🕐 30 mins

  COOK'S TIP

If you are making this dish for small children, the chicken can be finely chopped or minced first.

This quick and simple dish is colourful and healthy. It is perfect for an light lunch or supper dish.

Chicken *with* Red *and* Yellow Sauces

1 Heat 1 tablespoon of oil in each of 2 medium-sized saucepans. Place half of the onions, 1 garlic clove, red peppers, cayenne pepper and tomato purée in one saucepan. Place the remaining onion, garlic, yellow peppers and basil in the other pan.

2 Cover each pan and cook over a very low heat for 1 hour, until the peppers have softened. If either mixture becomes dry, add a little water. Work each mixture separately in a food processor, then sieve separately.

3 Return the separate mixtures to the pans and season with salt and pepper to taste. The 2 sauces can be gently reheated while the chicken is cooking.

4 Put the chicken breasts into a frying pan and add the wine and stock. Add the bouquet garni and bring the liquid to a simmer. Cook the chicken for about 20 minutes, until tender. Remove the bouquet garni.

5 To serve, pour a serving of each sauce on to 4 serving plates, slice the chicken breasts and arrange on the plates. Garnish with fresh herbs.

SERVES 4

2 tbsp olive oil
2 onions, finely chopped
2 garlic cloves, crushed
2 red peppers, deseeded and chopped
good pinch of cayenne pepper
2 tsp tomato purée
2 yellow peppers, deseeded and chopped
pinch of dried basil
4 skinless, boneless chicken breasts
150 ml/5 fl oz dry white wine
150 ml/5 fl oz chicken stock
bouquet garni, fresh or dried
salt and pepper
fresh herbs, to garnish

NUTRITION
Calories *257*; Sugars *7 g*; Protein *29 g*; Carbohydrate *8 g*; Fat *10 g*; Saturates *2 g*

  moderate

30 mins

1 hr 35 mins

COOK'S TIP

If you do not have time to make your own fresh or dried bouquet garni (see page 14), use a bouquet garni herb sachet.

Pâté is easy to make at home, and this combination of lean chicken and ham mixed with herbs is especially straightforward.

Parsley, Chicken *and* Ham Pâté

SERVES 4

225 g/8 oz cooked skinless, boneless chicken, diced
100 g/3½ oz lean ham, diced
small bunch of fresh parsley
1 tsp grated lime rind, plus extra to garnish
2 tbsp lime juice
1 garlic clove
125 ml/4 fl oz low-fat natural fromage frais
salt and pepper

to serve
lime wedges
crispbread or Melba toast
green salad

1 Place the chicken and ham in a blender or food processor.

2 Add the parsley, lime rind and juice, and garlic and process until finely minced. (Alternatively, finely chop the chicken, ham, parsley and garlic and place in a bowl. Gently stir in the lime rind and lime juice.)

3 Transfer the mixture to a bowl and stir in the fromage frais. Season with salt and pepper to taste, cover with clingfilm and chill in the refrigerator for about 30 minutes.

4 Spoon the pâté into individual serving dishes and garnish with extra grated lime rind. Serve the pâté with lime wedges, crispbread and a green salad.

NUTRITION
Calories *119*; Sugars *2 g*; Protein *20 g*;
Carbohydrate *2 g*; Fat *3 g*; Saturates *1 g*

⭐ very easy
🍴 45 mins
🕐 0 mins

👑 **COOK'S TIP**

This pâté can be made successfully with other kinds of minced, lean, cooked meat, such as turkey, beef and pork. Alternatively, replace the meat with peeled prawns and/or white crab meat, or with canned tuna in brine, drained.

Cooked potatoes and chicken are combined to make tasty nutty rissoles, which are served with stir-fried vegetables.

Chicken *and* Almond Rissoles

1 Combine the potatoes, carrot and chicken with the garlic, herbs and spices and season with salt and pepper to taste.

2 Add the egg and bind the ingredients together. Divide the mixture in half and shape into 'sausages'. Spread the almonds on a plate and coat each rissole in the nuts. Place the rissoles in a greased ovenproof dish and cook in a preheated oven, 200°C/400°F/Gas Mark 6, for about 20 minutes, until browned.

3 To stir-fry the vegetables, heat the oil in a frying pan and toss in the vegetables. Cook over a high heat for 1–2 minutes, then add the baby corn cobs and mangetout and cook for 2–3 minutes. Add the balsamic vinegar.

4 Serve the rissoles with the stir-fried vegetables and garnish with the lime wedges.

S E R V E S **4**

115 g/4 oz parboiled potatoes, grated
1 carrot, grated
115 g/4 oz cooked chicken, finely chopped or minced
1 garlic clove, crushed
½ tsp dried tarragon or thyme
pinch of ground allspice or ground coriander
1 egg yolk or ½ egg, beaten
about 25 g/1 oz flaked almonds, finely chopped
salt and pepper
lime wedges, to garnish

stir-fried vegetables

1 tbsp groundnut oil
1 celery stick, sliced thinly diagonally
2 spring onions, sliced thinly diagonally
8 baby corn cobs, sliced diagonally
40 g/1½ oz mangetout or sugar snap peas
2 tsp balsamic vinegar

N U T R I T I O N
Calories *161*; Sugars *3 g*; Protein *12 g*;
Carbohydrate *8 g*; Fat *9 g*; Saturates *1 g*

 moderate

 35 mins

35 mins

30 mins

Quick Dishes

When chicken is cut into small pieces it can be cooked very quickly, which is welcome for those of us who are too busy to spend a lot of time preparing meals. In this section you will find many tasty, nutritious dishes that won't take hours to make. Pasta makes a perfect partner for chicken as it is also quick to cook – Italian Chicken Spirals looks impressive and will fool guests into thinking that you have spent hours in the kitchen. Chicken breasts are also cooked with a creamy ricotta, spinach and garlic filling and then served on a bed of pasta. Smaller cuts of chicken are ideal for quick-cook stir-fries, to produce tender, moist and flavoursome chicken. Peanut Chicken with Noodles is a crunchy stir-fry that is served with thread egg noodles. Risottos are also an excellent choice for when you are in a hurry – this chapter contains two risotto recipes although the variations for risotto are almost endless!

This famous dish is one of many variations of what is perhaps the best known of all the Italian risottos.

Chicken Risotto *à la* Milanese

SERVES 4

125 g/4½ oz butter
900 g/2 lb chicken meat, sliced thinly
1 large onion, chopped
500 g/1 lb 2 oz arborio rice
600 ml/1 pint chicken stock
150 ml/5 fl oz white wine
1 tsp crumbled saffron strands
salt and pepper
55 g/2 oz Parmesan cheese, grated, to serve

1 Heat 55 g/2 oz of the butter in a heavy-based saucepan, and fry the chicken and onion until golden brown.

2 Add the rice, stir well, and cook for 15 minutes.

3 Heat the stock until boiling and gradually add to the rice. Add the white wine and saffron, and season with salt and pepper to taste, then mix well. Simmer gently for 20 minutes, stirring occasionally, adding more stock if the risotto becomes too dry.

4 Leave to stand for a few minutes and just before serving add a little more stock and simmer for a further 10 minutes. Serve the risotto, sprinkled with the Parmesan cheese and stir in the remaining butter.

NUTRITION
Calories *857*; Sugars *1 g*; Protein *57 g*;
Carbohydrate *72 g*; Fat *38 g*; Saturates *21 g*

 easy

15 mins

1 hr

COOK'S TIP

A risotto should be moist and creamy but have separate grains. The stock is usually added a little at a time and only when the last addition has been completely absorbed, but it can be added all at once if you are in a rush.

Chicken is surprisingly delicious when combined with fruit, such as grapes or gooseberries.

Chicken *and* Cream Sauce

1 Heat the butter and sunflower oil in a large, flameproof casserole or saucepan and quickly fry the chicken breasts until golden brown, turning once. Remove the chicken breasts and keep warm.

2 Add the shallots to the pan and fry gently until softened and lightly browned. Return the chicken breasts to the pan.

3 Add the chicken stock and cider vinegar to the pan, then bring to the boil. Reduce the heat, cover and simmer for 10–12 minutes, stirring occasionally.

4 Transfer the chicken to a serving dish. Add the grapes, cream and nutmeg to the pan. Heat through, then season with salt and pepper to taste. Add a little cornflour to thicken the sauce, if using. Pour the sauce over the chicken and serve immediately.

SERVES 4

15 g/½ oz butter
1 tbsp sunflower oil
4 skinless, boneless chicken breasts
4 shallots, chopped finely
150 ml/5 fl oz chicken stock
1 tbsp cider vinegar
175 g/6 oz white seedless grapes, halved
120 ml/4 fl oz double cream
1 tsp freshly grated nutmeg
salt and pepper
cornflour, for thickening (optional)

NUTRITION
Calories 351; Sugars 8 g; Protein 31 g;
Carbohydrate 5 g; Fat 22 g; Saturates 12 g

 COOK'S TIP

If desired, add a little dry white wine or vermouth to the sauce in step 3.

⭐⭐   easy

🕐   15 mins

🕐   30 mins

A complete main course which is cooked within 10 minutes. Thread egg noodles are the ideal accompaniment as they can be cooked quickly while the stir-fry sizzles.

Peanut Chicken *with* Noodles

SERVES 4

250 g/9 oz dried thread egg noodles
2 tbsp corn oil
1 tbsp sesame oil
8 boneless chicken thighs or 4 breasts, sliced thinly
300 g/10½ oz courgettes, thinly sliced
250 g/9 oz baby sweetcorn, sliced thinly
300 g/10½ oz button mushrooms, sliced thinly
350 g/12 oz beansprouts
4 tbsp smooth peanut butter
2 tbsp soy sauce
2 tbsp lime or lemon juice
55 g/2 oz roasted peanuts
pepper
sprigs of fresh coriander, to garnish

1 Bring a large saucepan of lightly salted boiling water to the boil and cook the noodles for 3–4 minutes. Drain the noodles.

2 Meanwhile, heat the corn oil and sesame oil in a large, heavy-based frying pan or preheated wok and fry the chicken over a fairly high heat for 1 minute. Add the courgettes, sweetcorn and button mushrooms and stir-fry for 5 minutes.

3 Add the beansprouts, peanut butter, soy sauce and lime juice and season with pepper to taste, then cook for a further 2 minutes.

4 Transfer the noodles to a serving dish and scatter with the roasted peanuts. Serve with the stir-fried chicken and vegetables, garnished with a sprig of coriander.

NUTRITION
Calories *563*; Sugars *7 g*; Protein *45 g*; Carbohydrate *22 g*; Fat *33 g*; Saturates *7 g*

 easy

 10 mins

15 mins

 **COOK'S TIP**

Try serving this stir-fry with rice sticks. These are broad, pale, translucent ribbon noodles made from ground rice.

Chicken breasts are stuffed with creamy ricotta, nutmeg and spinach, then wrapped in thin slices of Parma ham and gently cooked in white wine.

Parma-wrapped Chicken Cushions

1 Put the spinach into a sieve and press out the water with a spoon. Mix with the ricotta and nutmeg and season with salt and pepper to taste.

2 Using a sharp knife, slit each chicken breast through the side and enlarge each cut to form a pocket. Fill with the spinach mixture, reshape the chicken breasts, wrap each breast tightly in a slice of ham and secure with cocktail sticks. Cover and chill in the refrigerator.

3 Heat the butter and oil in a heavy-based frying pan and brown the chicken breasts for 2 minutes on each side. Transfer the chicken to a large, shallow ovenproof dish and keep warm until required.

4 Fry the onions and mushrooms for 2–3 minutes, until lightly browned. Stir in the plain flour then gradually add the wine and stock. Bring to the boil, stirring constantly. Season and spoon the mixture around the chicken.

5 Cook the chicken, uncovered, in a preheated oven, 200°C/400°F/Gas Mark 6, for 20 minutes. Turn the breasts over and cook for a further 10 minutes. Remove the cocktail sticks and serve with the sauce, together with carrot purée and French beans.

SERVES 4

125 g/4½ oz frozen spinach, defrosted
125 g/4½ oz ricotta cheese
pinch of grated nutmeg
4 skinless, boneless chicken breasts, about
    175 g/6 oz each
4 Parma ham slices
25 g/1 oz butter
1 tbsp olive oil
12 small onions or shallots
125 g/4½ oz button mushrooms, sliced
1 tbsp plain flour
150 ml/5 fl oz dry white or red wine
300 ml/5 fl oz chicken stock
salt and pepper

to serve
carrot purée
French beans

NUTRITION
Calories *609*; Sugars *11 g*; Protein *26 g*;
Carbohydrate *45 g*; Fat *38 g*; Saturates *6 g*

⚜⚜⚜   moderate
    20 mins
    40 mins

64

CHICKEN

These chicken breasts are served with a rich, velvety sauce made from whisky and crème fraîche.

Breast *of* Chicken *with* Whisky Sauce

SERVES 6

25 g/1 oz butter
55 g/2 oz leeks, shredded
55 g/2 oz carrot, diced
55 g/2 oz celery, diced
4 shallots, sliced
600 ml/1 pint chicken stock
6 chicken breasts
50 ml/2 fl oz whisky
200 ml/7 fl oz crème fraîche
2 tbsp freshly grated horseradish
1 tsp clear honey, warmed
1 tsp chopped fresh parsley
salt and pepper
sprigs of fresh parsley, to garnish

to serve
vegetable patties
steamed carrots

NUTRITION
Calories *337*; Sugars *6 g*; Protein *37 g*;
Carbohydrate *6 g*; Fat *15 g*; Saturates *8 g*

easy
20 mins
45 mins

1 Melt the butter in a large saucepan and add the leeks, carrot, celery and shallots. Cook for 3 minutes, add half of the chicken stock and cook for about 8 minutes.

2 Add the remaining chicken stock, bring to the boil, add the chicken breasts and cook for 10 minutes.

3 Remove the chicken and slice thinly. Place on a large, hot serving dish and keep warm until required.

4 In another saucepan, heat the whisky until reduced by half. Strain the chicken stock through a fine sieve, add to the pan and cook until the liquid has reduced by half.

5 Add the crème fraîche, horseradish and honey. Heat gently and add the chopped parsley and season with salt and pepper to taste. Stir until well blended.

6 Pour a little of the whisky sauce around the chicken and pour the remaining sauce into a sauceboat to serve.

7 Serve with vegetable patties made from the leftover vegetables, mashed potato and fresh vegetables. Garnish with parsley sprigs.

This subtly spiced chicken, spiked with cayenne pepper and paprika, is served in a fruity sauce.

Creamy Paprika Chicken

1 Mix the flour, cayenne pepper and paprika together in a dish and use to coat the chicken. Shake off any excess flour.

2 Melt the butter in a saucepan and gently fry the chicken with the onion for 4 minutes.

3 Stir in the flour and spice mixture. Add the milk slowly, stirring until the sauce thickens. Simmer until the sauce is smooth.

4 Add the apple purée and grapes and simmer gently for 20 minutes.

5 Transfer the chicken and devilled sauce to a serving dish and top with soured cream and a sprinkling of paprika.

SERVES 2 – 3

25 g/1 oz plain flour
1 tbsp cayenne pepper
1 tsp paprika
350 g/12 oz skinless, boneless chicken, diced
25 g/1 oz butter
1 onion, chopped finely
450 ml/16 fl oz milk, warmed
4 tbsp apple purée
125 g/4½ oz white grapes
150 ml/5 fl oz soured cream
sprinkle of paprika

NUTRITION
Calories *455*; Sugars *19 g*; Protein *37 g*;
Carbohydrate *29 g*; Fat *23 g*; Saturates *14 g*

 very easy
 10 mins
 35 mins

🍴 COOK'S TIP

Since paprika is quite a mild spice, you can add more to this dish without it becoming too overpowering, if liked.

CHICKEN

Steaming allows you to cook without fat, and these little foil parcels retain all the natural juices of the chicken.

Italian Chicken Spirals

SERVES 4

4 skinless, boneless chicken breasts
25 g/1 oz fresh basil leaves
15 g/½ oz hazelnuts
1 garlic clove, crushed
250 g/9 oz dried wholemeal pasta spirals
2 sun-dried tomatoes or fresh tomatoes, diced
1 tbsp lemon juice
1 tbsp olive oil
1 tbsp capers
55 g/2 oz black olives
salt and pepper

1 Beat the chicken breasts with a rolling pin to flatten evenly.

2 Place the basil and hazelnuts in a food processor and process until finely chopped. Mix with the garlic, and season with salt and pepper to taste.

3 Spread the basil mixture over the chicken breasts and roll up from one short end to enclose the filling. Wrap the chicken roll tightly in foil so that they hold their shape, then seal the ends well.

4 Bring a large saucepan of lightly salted water to the boil and cook the pasta until tender, but still firm to the bite.

5 Place the chicken parcels in a steamer basket or colander set over the pan, cover tightly, and steam for 10 minutes.

6 Drain the pasta and return it to the pan with the lemon juice, olive oil, tomatoes, capers and olives, then heat through.

7 To ensure the chicken is cooked, pierce the thickest part with a skewer to make sure that the juices run clear and not pink. Slice the chicken, arrange over the pasta and serve.

NUTRITION
Calories *367*; Sugars *1 g*; Protein *33 g*;
Carbohydrate *35 g*; Fat *12 g*; Saturates *2 g*

 ❂❂❂   moderate
🕐   25 mins
🕐   20 mins

🏅 **COOK'S TIP**

Sun-dried tomatoes have a wonderful, rich flavour, but if you can't find them use fresh tomatoes instead.

Stuffed with creamy ricotta, spinach and garlic, the chicken is gently cooked in a rich tomato sauce. This is an ideal dish to make in advance.

Ricotta-stuffed Chicken *with* Tomato

1 Make a slit between the skin and meat on one side of each chicken breast. Lift the skin to form a pocket, being careful to leave the skin attached to the other side.

2 Put the spinach into a sieve and press out the water with a spoon. Mix with the ricotta and half of the garlic then season with salt and pepper to taste.

3 Spoon the spinach mixture under the skin of each chicken breast then secure the edge of the skin with cocktail sticks.

4 Heat the oil in a heavy-based frying pan, add the onion and fry for a minute, stirring. Add the remaining garlic and red pepper and cook for 2 minutes. Stir in the tomatoes, wine, olives and seasoning. (Set the sauce aside and chill the chicken if preparing in advance.)

5 Bring the sauce to the boil, pour into a shallow ovenproof dish and arrange the chicken breasts on top in a single layer.

6 Cook, uncovered in a preheated oven, 200°C/400°F/Gas Mark 6, for 35 minutes, until the chicken is golden and cooked through. Test by making a slit in one of the chicken breasts with a skewer to make sure the juices run clear and not pink. Spoon a little of the sauce over the chicken breasts, then transfer to serving plates. Serve with pasta.

SERVES 4

4 part-boned chicken breasts
125 g/4½ oz frozen spinach, defrosted
150 g/5½ oz ricotta cheese
2 garlic cloves, crushed
1 tbsp olive oil
1 onion, chopped
1 red pepper, deseeded and sliced
400 g/14 oz canned chopped tomatoes
6 tbsp wine or chicken stock
10 stuffed olives, sliced
salt and pepper
pasta, to serve

NUTRITION
Calories *316*; Sugars *6 g*; Protein *40 g*; Carbohydrate *6 g*; Fat *13 g*; Saturates *5 g*

  moderate

20 mins

  45 mins

Very simple to make and
easy to eat with the
fingers, this dish can be
served warm for a light
lunch or cold as part of
a buffet party.

Chicken Strips *and* Dips

S E R V E S   2

2 skinless, boneless chicken breasts, cut into
   thin strips
15 g/½ oz plain flour
1 tbsp sunflower oil
assorted vegetable sticks, to serve

peanut dip
3 tbsp smooth or crunchy peanut butter
4 tbsp natural yogurt
1 tsp grated orange rind
orange juice (optional)

tomato dip
1 tomato, chopped
5 tbsp creamy fromage frais
2 tsp tomato purée
1 tsp chopped fresh chives

1 Toss the chicken in the flour to coat.

2 Heat the oil in a heavy-based frying pan and cook the chicken until golden
  and thoroughly cooked. Remove the chicken strips from the pan and drain
  well on kitchen paper.

3 To make the peanut dip, mix together all the ingredients in a bowl. Add a
  little orange juice to thin the consistency, if liked.

4 Mix together all the ingredients for the tomato dip.

5 Serve the chicken strips with the dips and vegetable sticks for dipping.

N U T R I T I O N
Calories *575*; Sugars *16 g*; Protein *50 g*;
Carbohydrate *24 g*; Fat *32 g*; Saturates *10 g*

 easy

🕐 20 mins

🕐 10 mins

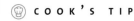 **C O O K ' S   T I P**

For a lower-fat alternative, poach the strips of chicken in a small amount of
boiling chicken stock for 6–8 minutes.

If preferred, use boneless chicken breasts in this recipe. This dish incorporates a surprising combination of coffee liqueur and brandy.

Flambéed Chicken

1 Place the chicken breasts or suprêmes on a chopping board, cover with clingfilm and pound them until flattened with a wooden meat mallet or a rolling pin.

2 Heat the oil in a large, heavy-based frying pan and fry the chicken for 3 minutes on each side. Add the shallots and cook for a further 3 minutes.

3 Sprinkle with the lemon juice and lemon rind and add the Worcestershire sauce and chicken stock. Cook for 2 minutes, then sprinkle with the chopped fresh parsley.

4 Add the coffee liqueur and brandy and flame the chicken by lighting the spirit with a taper or long match. Cook until the flame has extinguished, then serve.

SERVES 4

4 chicken breasts or suprêmes, about
    125 g/4½ oz each
4 tbsp corn oil
8 shallots, sliced
rind and juice of 1 lemon
2 tsp Worcestershire sauce
4 tbsp chicken stock
1 tbsp chopped fresh parsley
3 tbsp coffee liqueur
3 tbsp brandy, warmed

NUTRITION
Calories *294*; Sugars *5 g*; Protein *30 g*;
Carbohydrate *6 g*; Fat *12 g*; Saturates *2 g*

 challenging
 10 mins
10 mins
15 mins

🍴 COOK'S TIP

A suprême is a chicken fillet that sometimes has part of the wing bone remaining. Chicken breasts can be used instead.

A sweet and fruity glaze coats the chicken breasts in this tasty recipe. The minty rice makes the dish complete.

Golden Glazed Chicken

SERVES **6**

6 boneless chicken breasts
1 tsp turmeric
1 tbsp wholegrain mustard
300 ml/10 fl oz orange juice
2 tbsp clear honey
2 tbsp sunflower oil
350 g/12 oz long-grain rice
1 orange
3 tbsp chopped fresh mint
salt and pepper
sprigs of fresh mint, to garnish

1 With a sharp knife, mark the surface of the chicken breasts in a diamond pattern. Mix together the turmeric, mustard, orange juice and honey and pour it over the chicken. Chill until required.

2 Lift the chicken from the marinade and pat dry with kitchen paper.

3 Heat the oil in a frying pan, add the chicken and sauté until golden, turning once. Drain off any excess oil. Pour the marinade over, cover and simmer for 10–15 minutes, until the chicken is tender.

4 Boil the rice in lightly salted water until tender and drain well. Finely grate the rind from the orange and stir into the rice with the mint.

5 Using a sharp knife, remove the peel and white pith from the orange and cut the flesh into segments.

6 Serve the chicken with the orange and mint rice, garnished with orange segments and mint sprigs.

NUTRITION
Calories *427*; Sugars *11 g*; Protein *39 g*;
Carbohydrate *42 g*; Fat *12 g*; Saturates *3 g*

 moderate
5 mins
 35 mins

COOK'S TIP

For a slightly sharper flavour, use the grated rind of a small grapefruit in the rice instead of the oranges.

Cooking the chicken in foil parcels makes it aromatic and succulent. It also reduces the amount of oil needed, since the chicken and vegetables cook in their own juices.

Mediterranean Chicken Parcels

1 Cut 6 pieces of foil, each about 25-cm/10-inches square. Brush the foil squares lightly with oil and set aside until required.

2 With a sharp knife, slash each chicken breast at intervals, then place the mozzarella between the cuts in the chicken.

3 Divide the courgettes and tomatoes between the pieces of foil and season with black pepper to taste. Scatter the basil over the vegetables in each parcel.

4 Place the chicken on top of each pile of vegetables, then wrap in the foil to enclose the chicken and vegetables, tucking in the ends.

5 Place on a baking tray and bake in a preheated oven, 200°C/400°C/Gas Mark 6, for about 30 minutes.

6 To serve, unwrap each foil parcel and serve with pasta or rice.

SERVES 6

1 tbsp olive oil
6 skinless chicken breasts
250 g/9 oz mozzarella cheese, sliced
500 g/1 lb 2 oz courgettes, sliced
6 large tomatoes, sliced
1 small bunch of fresh basil or oregano, leaves torn
pepper
pasta or rice, to serve

NUTRITION
Calories 234; Sugars 5 g; Protein 28 g;
Carbohydrate 5 g; Fat 12 g; Saturates 5 g

 easy

25 mins

 30 mins

🍳 **COOK'S TIP**

Place the vegetables and chicken on the shiny side of the foil so the dull surface of the foil is facing outwards. This ensures that the heat is absorbed into the parcel and not reflected away from it.

This quick and healthy stir-fry uses only the minimum of fat. If you don't have a wok, use a wide, heavy-based frying pan instead.

Caramelised Chicken Stir-fry

SERVES 4

2 tbsp sunflower oil
4 skinless, boneless chicken breasts, cut into thin strips
250 g/9 oz baby corn cobs, halved lengthways
250 g/9 oz mangetout
1 tbsp sherry vinegar
1 tbsp honey
1 tbsp light soy sauce
1 tbsp sunflower seeds
pepper
egg noodles, to serve

1 Heat the sunflower oil in a preheated wok or a large, heavy-based frying pan and stir-fry the chicken over a fairly high heat, stirring constantly, for 1 minute.

2 Add the corn cobs and mangetout and stir-fry over a moderate heat for 5–8 minutes, until evenly cooked.

3 Mix together the sherry vinegar, honey and soy sauce and stir into the pan with the sunflower seeds. Season with pepper to taste. Cook, stirring constantly, for 1 minute. Serve hot with Chinese egg noodles.

NUTRITION

Calories *280*; Sugars *7 g*; Protein *31 g*; Carbohydrate *9 g*; Fat *11 g*; Saturates *2 g*

⭐ very easy
🕐 5 mins
🕐 10 mins

 COOK'S TIP

Rice vinegar or balsamic vinegar makes a good substitute for the sherry vinegar in this recipe.

Served with a smooth creamy tomato sauce, these chicken bites make an excellent light lunch with freshly baked cheesy bread.

Crispy-coated Chicken Morsels

1 In a large clean bowl, combine the breadcrumbs, chicken, leek, mixed herbs and mustard powder, and season with salt and pepper to taste. Mix together until thoroughly blended.

2 Add 1 whole egg and an egg yolk with a little milk to bind the mixture.

3 Divide the mixture into 6 or 8 and shape into thick or thin sausages.

4 Whisk the remaining egg white until frothy. Coat the sausages first in the egg white and then in the crisp breadcrumbs.

5 Heat the dripping and fry the sausages for 6 minutes, until golden brown. Serve with the tomatoes and roast potatoes.

SERVES 6

175 g/6 oz fresh breadcrumbs
250 g/9 oz cooked chicken, minced
1 small leek, chopped finely
pinch each of mixed herbs and mustard powder
2 eggs, separated
4 tbsp milk
crisp breadcrumbs, for coating
25 g/1 oz beef dripping
salt and pepper
sprigs of fresh parsley, to garnish

to serve
tomatoes, halved
roast potatoes

NUTRITION
Calories *268*; Sugars *2 g*; Protein *18 g*; Carbohydrate *27 g*; Fat *10 g*; Saturates *4 g*

moderate
15 mins
10 mins

👨‍🍳 COOK'S TIP

Make your own minced chicken by working lean cuts of chicken through a food processor.

If preferred, ordinary long-grain rice can be used instead of arborio rice, but it won't give you the traditional, deliciously creamy texture that is typical of Italian risottos.

Italian Risotto

SERVES 4

2 tbsp sunflower oil
15 g/½ oz butter or margarine
1 leek, thinly sliced
1 large yellow pepper, deseeded and diced
3 skinless, boneless chicken breasts, diced
350 g/12 oz arborio rice
few strands of saffron
1.5 litres/2¾ pints chicken stock
200 g/7 oz canned sweetcorn
55 g/2 oz toasted unsalted peanuts
55 g/2 oz grated Parmesan cheese
salt and pepper

1 Heat the oil and butter in a large, heavy-based saucepan. Add the leek and yellow pepper and cook for 1 minute. Add the chicken and cook, stirring, until golden brown.

2 Stir in the rice and cook for 2–3 minutes. Add the saffron strands and season with salt and pepper to taste.

3 Add the stock, a little at a time, and cook over a low heat, stirring continuously, for about 20 minutes, until the rice is tender and most of the liquid has been absorbed. Do not let the risotto dry out – add more stock, if necessary.

4 Stir in the sweetcorn, peanuts and Parmesan cheese, then adjust the seasoning to taste. Serve hot.

NUTRITION
Calories 701; Sugars 7 g; Protein 35 g;
Carbohydrate 88 g; Fat 26 g; Saturates 8 g

 easy

 10 mins

30 mins

 COOK'S TIP

Risottos can be frozen for up to 1 month before adding the Parmesan cheese, but remember to reheat this risotto thoroughly as it contains chicken.

This recipe is a version of the classic cottage pie, which is made with minced beef and is just as delicious. Add the vegetables and herbs of your choice, depending on what you have at hand.

Chicken Cottage Pie

1 Dry-fry the minced chicken, onion and carrots in a non-stick saucepan for 5 minutes, stirring frequently.

2 Sprinkle the chicken with the flour and simmer for a further 2 minutes.

3 Gradually blend in the tomato purée and stock, then simmer for 15 minutes. Season with salt and pepper to taste and add the thyme.

4 Transfer the chicken and vegetable mixture to an ovenproof casserole and allow to cool.

5 Spoon the mashed potato over the chicken and vegetable mixture and sprinkle with the Lancashire cheese. Bake in a preheated oven, 200°C/400°F/Gas Mark 6, for 20 minutes, or until the cheese is bubbling and golden, then serve with the peas.

SERVES 4

500 g/1 lb 2 oz minced chicken
1 large onion, chopped finely
2 carrots, diced finely
25 g/1 oz plain flour
1 tbsp tomato purée
300 ml/10 fl oz chicken stock
pinch of fresh thyme
900 g/2 lb potatoes, mashed with butter
   and milk and seasoned
85 g/3 oz Lancashire cheese, grated
salt and pepper
peas, to serve

NUTRITION
Calories *496*; Sugars *10 g*; Protein *38 g*;
Carbohydrate *52 g*; Fat *17 g*; Saturates *9 g*

⭐⭐⭐   moderate
🕐   25 mins
🕐   45 mins

 COOK'S TIP

Instead of Lancashire cheese, you could sprinkle Cotswold cheese over the top. This is a tasty blend of Double Gloucester, onion and chives, and is ideal for melting as a topping.

This unusual recipe uses chicken and Cumberland sausage, cooked in a light batter and served with a rich gravy.

Chicken Toad-in-the-hole

SERVES 4 – 6

125 g/4½ oz plain flour
pinch of salt
1 egg, beaten
200 ml/7 fl oz milk
90 ml/3 fl oz water
2 tbsp beef dripping
250 g/9 oz chicken breasts, cut into thick chunks
250 g/9 oz Cumberland sausage, cut into thick chunks

to serve
steamed cabbage
chicken or onion gravy

1 Mix together the flour and salt in a bowl, make a well in the centre and add the beaten egg.

2 Add half of the milk and, using a wooden spoon, work in the flour slowly.

3 Beat the mixture until smooth, then add the remaining milk and water.

4 Beat again until the mixture is smooth. Leave the mixture to stand for at least 1 hour.

5 Add the dripping to individual baking tins or to one large baking tin. Place a piece of chicken and sausage in each individual tin or arrange several pieces around the large tin.

6 Heat in a preheated oven, 220°C/425°F/Gas Mark 7, for 5 minutes, until very hot. Remove the tins from the oven and pour in the batter, leaving space for the mixture to expand.

7 Return to the oven to cook for 35 minutes, until risen and golden brown. (Do not open the oven door for at least 30 minutes.)

8 Serve hot, with cabbage and gravy, if using.

NUTRITION
Calories *470*; Sugars *4 g*; Protein *28 g*;
Carbohydrate *30 g*; Fat *27 g*; Saturates *12 g*

easy

1 hr 15 mins

30 mins

 COOK'S TIP

Skinless, boneless chicken legs can be used instead of the chicken breasts in this recipe. Your favourite variety of sausage can also replace the Cumberland sausage, if liked.

Low in fat and high in fibre, this colourful casserole makes a healthy and hearty meal for a cold winter's day.

Chicken *and* Cannellini Bean Casserole

1 Toss the chicken drumsticks in the flour to coat evenly. Heat the oil in a heavy-based saucepan and fry the chicken over a fairly high heat, turning frequently, until golden brown. Transfer to a large casserole and keep warm until required.

2 Add the onions to the pan and cook for a few minutes until lightly browned. Stir in the garlic.

3 Add the fennel seeds, bay leaf, orange rind and juice, tomatoes, and beans, and season with salt and pepper to taste.

4 Cover and cook in a preheated oven, 190°C/375°F/ Gas Mark 5, for 30–35 minutes, until the chicken juices are clear and not pink when it is pierced through the thickest part with a skewer.

5 For the topping, toss the bread in the oil. Remove the lid from the casserole and top with the bread cubes. Bake for a further 15–20 minutes, until the bread is golden and crisp. Serve hot.

SERVES 4

8 skinless chicken drumsticks
1 tbsp wholemeal flour
1 tbsp olive oil
2 red onions, cut into thin wedges
1 garlic clove, crushed
1 tsp fennel seeds
1 bay leaf
finely grated rind and juice of 1 small orange
400 g/14 oz canned chopped tomatoes
400 g/14 oz canned cannellini or flageolet beans, drained and rinsed
3 thick slices wholemeal bread, diced
2 tsp olive oil
salt and pepper

NUTRITION
Calories *345*; Sugars *6 g*; Protein *29 g*; Carbohydrate *39 g*; Fat *10 g*; Saturates *2 g*

 moderate
 10 mins
1 hr

🍲 **COOK'S TIP**

Choose beans which are canned in water with no added sugar or salt. Drain and rinse well before use.

A healthy recipe with a
delicate Oriental flavour.
Use large spinach leaves
to wrap around the
chicken, but make sure
they are young and tender.

Steamed Chicken Parcels

SERVES 4

4 skinless, boneless chicken breasts
1 tsp ground lemon grass
2 spring onions, finely chopped
250 g/9 oz young carrots, cut into small batons
250 g/9 oz young courgettes, cut into small batons
2 celery sticks, cut into small batons
1 tsp light soy sauce
250 g/9 oz spinach leaves, rinsed and drained
2 tsp sesame oil
salt and pepper

1 With a sharp knife, make a slit through 1 side of each chicken breast to make a large pocket.

2 Sprinkle the inside of the pocket with lemon grass and season with salt and pepper to taste. Tuck the spring onions into the chicken pockets.

3 Blanch the vegetables into a pan of boiling water for 1 minute, then drain and toss in the soy sauce.

4 Fill the pockets in each chicken breast with the vegetable mixture, but do not over-stuff. Fold over firmly to enclose. Reserve the remaining vegetables.

5 Wrap the chicken breasts firmly in the spinach leaves to enclose completely. If the leaves are too firm, steam them gently for a few seconds until they have softened and become flexible.

6 Place the wrapped chicken in a steamer and cook over rapidly boiling water for 20–25 minutes, until tender and cooked through.

7 Stir-fry any leftover vegetable batons and spinach for 1–2 minutes in the sesame oil and serve with the chicken.

NUTRITION
Calories 216; Sugars 7 g; Protein 31 g;
Carbohydrate 7 g; Fat 7 g; Saturates 2 g

 challenging
20 mins
 30 mins

This sweet-sour citrus chicken is delicious hot or cold. Sesame-flavoured noodles are the ideal accompaniment for the hot version.

Sweet-Sour Chicken

1 Using a sharp knife, score the chicken breasts with a criss-cross pattern on both sides (making sure that you do not cut all the way through the meat).

2 Combine the honey, soy sauce, lemon rind and juice in a small bowl and season with black pepper.

3 Arrange the chicken breasts on the grill rack and brush with half of the honey mixture. Cook under a preheated grill for 10 minutes, then turn over and brush with the remaining mixture. Cook for a further 8–10 minutes, or until cooked through and tender. The juices should run clear when pierced with a skewer.

4 Meanwhile, prepare the noodles, according to the instructions on the packet. Drain well and transfer to a warm serving bowl. Add the sesame oil, sesame seeds and lemon rind and toss well to mix. Season with salt and pepper to taste and keep warm.

5 Serve the chicken with a small mound of noodles, garnished with chives and lemon rind.

SERVES 4

4 skinless, boneless chicken breasts, about 125 g/4½ oz each
2 tbsp clear honey
1 tbsp dark soy sauce
1 tsp finely grated lemon rind
1 tbsp lemon juice
salt and pepper

to serve
225 g/8 oz rice noodles
2 tsp sesame oil
1 tbsp sesame seeds
1 tsp finely grated lemon rind

to garnish
1 tbsp chopped fresh chives
grated lemon rind

NUTRITION
Calories 248; Sugars 8 g; Protein 30 g; Carbohydrate 16 g; Fat 8 g; Saturates 2 g

easy

5 mins

25 mins

A karahi is an extremely versatile two-handled metal pan, similar to a wok. Food is always cooked over a high heat in a karahi.

Karahi Chicken

SERVES 4

2 tbsp ghee
3 garlic cloves, crushed
1 onion, chopped finely
2 tbsp garam masala
1 tsp ground coriander
½ tsp dried mint
1 bay leaf
750 g/1 lb 10 oz skinless, boneless chicken, diced
200 ml/7 fl oz chicken stock
1 tbsp chopped fresh coriander
salt
warm naan bread or chapatis, to serve

1 Heat the ghee in a preheated karahi, wok or a large, heavy-based frying pan. Add the garlic and onion. Stir-fry for about 4 minutes, until the onion is golden.

2 Stir in the garam masala, ground coriander, mint and bay leaf.

3 Add the chicken and cook over a high heat, stirring occasionally, for about 5 minutes. Add the stock, reduce the heat and simmer for 10 minutes, until the sauce has thickened and the chicken juices run clear when the meat is pierced through the thickest part with a skewer.

4 Stir in the coriander and season with salt to taste, mix well and serve immediately with warm naan bread.

NUTRITION

Calories 270; Sugars 1 g; Protein 41 g;
Carbohydrate 1 g; Fat 11 g; Saturates 2 g

 easy

15 mins

20 mins

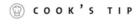 COOK'S TIP

Always heat a karahi or wok before you add the oil to help to maintain the high temperature.

This is quite a hot dish, using fresh chillies. If you prefer a milder dish, halve the number of chillies used.

Chilli Chicken

1 Place the chicken in a mixing bowl. Add the salt, egg white, cornflour and 1 tablespoon of the oil. Turn the chicken in the mixture to coat thoroughly.

2 Heat the remaining oil in a preheated wok or large, heavy-based frying pan. Add the garlic and ginger and stir-fry for 30 seconds.

3 Add the chicken to the wok and stir-fry for 2–3 minutes, until browned.

4 Stir in the peppers, chillies, soy sauce, sherry and wine vinegar and cook for a further 2–3 minutes, until the chicken is cooked through. Transfer to a warm serving dish and serve.

SERVES 4

350 g/12 oz skinless, boneless chicken, cubed
½ tsp salt
1 egg white, beaten lightly
2 tbsp cornflour
4 tbsp vegetable oil
2 garlic cloves, crushed
1-cm/½-inch piece of fresh root ginger, grated
1 red pepper, deseeded and diced
1 green pepper, deseeded and diced
2 fresh red chillies, chopped
2 tbsp light soy sauce
1 tbsp dry sherry or Chinese rice wine
1 tbsp wine vinegar

NUTRITION
Calories *265*; Sugars *3 g*; Protein *21 g*; Carbohydrate *11 g*; Fat *14 g*; Saturates *2 g*

 easy

10 mins

10 mins

 COOK'S TIP

When preparing chillies, wear rubber gloves to prevent the juices from burning and irritating your hands. Be careful not to touch your face, especially your lips or eyes, until you have washed your hands.

Casseroles *and* Roasts

Long slow-cooking means meltingly succulent meat with a good, rich flavour. Since chicken does not have a strong flavour, it marries happily with almost any other ingredient, herb or spice. The recipes in this section are drawn from many cuisines from around the world – there are dishes from Italy, France, Hungary, the Caribbean and the USA. French classics include Bourguignonne of Chicken and Brittany Chicken Casserole.

The aroma of roasting chicken is always tempting and this section includes the traditional roast with all the trimmings, as well as many other imaginative cooking ideas. Unusual stuffings to try are courgette and lime, marmalade, or oat and herb. Many of the recipes in this section exploit the complementary flavours of chicken and fruit and you will find some enticing taste combinations.

CHICKEN

Spices, herbs, fruit, nuts and vegetables are combined to make an appealing casserole with lots of flavour.

Chicken, Almond *and* Grape Casserole

SERVES 4 – 6

3 tbsp olive oil
900 g/2 lb chicken breasts, sliced
10 shallots or button onions
3 carrots, chopped
55 g/2 oz chestnuts, sliced
55 g/2 oz flaked almonds, toasted
1 tsp freshly grated nutmeg
3 tsp ground cinnamon
300 ml/10 fl oz white wine
300 ml/10 fl oz chicken stock
175 ml/6 fl oz white wine vinegar
1 tbsp chopped fresh tarragon
1 tbsp chopped fresh flat-leaved parsley
1 tbsp chopped fresh thyme
grated rind of 1 orange
1 tbsp dark muscovado sugar
125 g/4½ oz seedless black grapes, halved
sea salt and pepper
sprigs of fresh herbs, to garnish
wild rice or mashed potato, to serve

NUTRITION

Calories *385*; Sugars *14 g*; Protein *37 g*;
Carbohydrate *19 g*; Fat *15 g*; Saturates *2 g*

easy

15 mins

2 hrs 15 mins

1 Heat the olive oil in a large, heavy-based saucepan and fry the chicken, shallots and carrots for about 6 minutes, or until browned.

2 Add the remaining ingredients, except the grapes, and simmer over a low heat for 2 hours, until the meat is very tender. Stir the casserole occasionally.

3 Add the grapes just before serving. Garnish with the herbs and serve with the wild rice or mashed potato.

🍳 COOK'S TIP

This casserole is delicious served with thick slices of crusty wholemeal bread to soak up the sauce.

There are many regional versions of hotpot, all using fresh, local and seasonal ingredients. Now, there is an almost endless variety of ingredients available all year, perfect for traditional one-pot cooking.

Chicken *and* Herb Hotpot

1 Remove the skin from the chicken quarters, if preferred.

2 Arrange a layer of potato slices in the bottom of a wide casserole. Season with salt and pepper to taste, then add the thyme, rosemary and bay leaves.

3 Top with the chicken quarters, then sprinkle with the bacon, onion and carrots. Season well and arrange the remaining potato slices on top, overlapping slightly.

4 Pour over the stout, brush the potatoes with the melted butter and cover with a lid.

5 Bake in a preheated oven, 150°C/300°F/Gas Mark 2, for about 2 hours, removing the lid for the last 30 minutes to allow the potatoes to brown.

SERVES 4

4 chicken quarters
6 potatoes, cut into 5-mm/¼-inch slices
2 sprigs of fresh thyme
2 sprigs of fresh rosemary
2 bay leaves
200 g/7 oz rindless, smoked streaky bacon, diced
1 large onion, finely chopped
200 g/7 oz carrots, sliced
150 ml/5 fl oz stout
25 g/1 oz butter, melted
salt and pepper

NUTRITION
Calories *499*; Sugars *6 g*; Protein *43 g*; Carbohydrate *44 g*; Fat *17 g*; Saturates *8 g*

moderate

15 mins

2 hrs

 COOK'S TIP

This dish is also delicious with stewing lamb, cut into chunks. You can add different vegetables depending on what is in season – try leeks and swedes for a slightly sweeter flavour.

The addition of lime juice and lime rind adds a delicious tangy flavour to this chicken stew, while the peppers add a splash of colour.

Chicken *and* Lime stew

SERVES 4

1 chicken, weighing about 900 g/2lb, cut into small portions

55 g/2 oz flour, seasoned

2 tbsp oil

500 g/1 lb 2 oz button onions or shallots, sliced

1 each green and red pepper, deseeded and sliced thinly

150 ml/5 fl oz chicken stock

juice and rind of 2 limes

2 fresh chillies, chopped

2 tbsp oyster sauce

1 tsp Worcestershire sauce

salt and pepper

1 Coat the chicken pieces in the seasoned flour. Heat the oil in a large, heavy-based frying pan and cook the chicken for about 4 minutes, until browned.

2 Using a slotted spoon, transfer the chicken to a large casserole and sprinkle with the onions. Keep warm until required.

3 Cook the green and red peppers in the juices remaining in the frying pan.

4 Add the chicken stock, lime juice and rind and cook for a further 5 minutes.

5 Add the chillies, oyster sauce and Worcestershire sauce. Season with salt and pepper to taste.

6 Pour the peppers and juices over the chicken and onions. Cover the casserole with a lid or cooking foil.

7 Cook in the centre of a preheated oven, 190°C/375°F/Gas Mark 5, for 1½ hours, until the chicken is very tender, then serve.

NUTRITION

Calories *235*; Sugars *3 g*; Protein *20 g*; Carbohydrate *26 g*; Fat *6 g*; Saturates *1 g*

 moderate

 15 mins

1 hr 45 mins

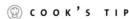 **COOK'S TIP**

Try this casserole with a cheese scone topping. About 30 minutes before the end of cooking time, simply top with rounds cut from cheese scone dough.

A recipe based on a classic French dish. Use a good quality wine when making this casserole.

Bourguignonne *of* Chicken

1 Heat the sunflower oil in an ovenproof casserole and brown the chicken all over. Remove from the casserole with a slotted spoon.

2 Add the mushrooms, bacon, shallots and garlic to the casserole and cook for 4 minutes.

3 Return the chicken to the casserole and sprinkle with flour. Cook for a further 2 minutes, stirring.

4 Add the Burgundy wine and chicken stock to the casserole and stir until boiling. Add the bouquet garni and season with salt and pepper to taste.

5 Cover the casserole and bake in the centre of a preheated oven, 150°C/300°F/Gas Mark 2, for 1½ hours. Remove the bouquet garni.

6 Deep-fry some heart-shaped croûtons (about 8 large ones) in beef dripping and serve with the bourguignonne and an assortment of vegetables.

SERVES 4 – 6

4 tbsp sunflower oil
900 g/2 lb chicken meat, diced
250 g/9 oz button mushrooms
125 g/4½ oz rindless, smoked bacon, diced
16 shallots
2 garlic cloves, crushed
1 tbsp plain flour
150 ml/5 fl oz white Burgundy wine
150 ml/5 fl oz chicken stock
1 fresh bouquet garni with sage and 1 celery stick
salt and pepper

to serve
deep-fried croûtons
assortment of vegetables

NUTRITION
Calories *476*; Sugars *3 g*; Protein *58 g*; Carbohydrate *8 g*; Fat *21 g*; Saturates *5 g*

moderate

15 mins

1 hr 30 mins

🖐 **COOK'S TIP**

A good-quality red wine can be used instead of the white wine, to produce a rich, glossy red sauce.

This economical bake is a complete meal – its herb-flavoured French bread topping mops up the tasty juices, and means there's no need to serve potatoes or rice separately.

Chicken, Bean *and* Celery Bake

SERVES 4

2 tbsp sunflower oil
4 chicken quarters
16 small whole onions, peeled
3 celery sticks, sliced
400 g/14 oz canned red kidney beans, drained and rinsed
4 tomatoes, quartered
200 ml/7 fl oz dry cider or chicken stock
4 tbsp chopped fresh parsley
salt and pepper
1 tsp paprika
55 g/2 oz butter
12 slices French bread

1 Heat the oil in a flameproof casserole and fry the chicken quarters, 2 at a time, until golden. Using a slotted spoon, remove the chicken from the pan and set aside until required.

2 Add the onions and fry, turning occasionally, until golden brown. Add the celery and fry for 2–3 minutes. Return the chicken to the pan, then stir in the beans, tomatoes, cider or stock, half of the parsley, and season with salt and pepper to taste. Sprinkle with the paprika.

3 Cover and cook in a preheated oven, 200°C/400°F/Gas Mark 6, for 20–25 minutes, until the juices run clear when the chicken is pierced through the thickest part with a skewer.

4 Mix the remaining parsley with the butter and spread evenly over the French bread slices.

5 Remove the lid of the casserole, arrange the bread slices overlapping on top and bake for a further 10–12 minutes, until golden and crisp.

NUTRITION
Calories *736*; Sugars *11 g*; Protein *50 g*; Carbohydrate *55 g*; Fat *35 g*; Saturates *13 g*

⭐⭐ easy
🕐 15 mins
🕐 1 hr

🎩 **COOK'S TIP**

For a more unusual Italian-tasting dish, replace the garlic and parsley bread topping with pesto-covered toasts.

Goulash is traditionally made with beef, but this recipe successfully uses chicken instead. To reduce the fat content, use a low-fat cream in place of the soured cream.

Goulash *with* Claret *and* Cream

1 Toss the chicken in the seasoned flour until it is coated all over.

2 In a flameproof casserole, heat the oil and butter and fry the onion, shallots and red and green peppers for 3 minutes.

3 Add the chicken and cook for a further 4 minutes. Sprinkle with the paprika and rosemary.

4 Add the tomato purée, chicken stock, claret and tomatoes, cover and cook in the centre of a preheated oven, 160°C/325°F/ Gas Mark 3, for 1½ hours.

5 Remove the casserole from the oven, allow it to stand for 4 minutes, then add the soured cream and garnish with parsley.

6 Serve with chunks of bread and a mixed salad.

SERVES 6

900 g/1¾ lb skinless chicken meat, diced
55 g/2 oz flour, seasoned with 1 tsp paprika, salt and pepper
2 tbsp olive oil
25 g/1 oz butter
1 onion, sliced
24 shallots, peeled
1 each red and green pepper, deseeded and chopped
1 tbsp paprika
1 tsp dried rosemary
4 tbsp tomato purée
300 ml/10 fl oz chicken stock
150 ml/5 fl oz claret
400 g/14 oz canned chopped tomatoes
150 ml/5 fl oz soured cream
1 tbsp chopped fresh parsley, to garnish

to serve
chunks of bread
mixed salad

NUTRITION

Calories *509*; Sugars *12 g*; Protein *46 g*; Carbohydrate *26 g*; Fat *32 g*; Saturates *10 g*

 moderate

 20 mins

1 hr 45 mins

 COOK'S TIP

Serve the goulash with buttered ribbon noodles instead of bread. For an authentic touch, try a Hungarian red wine instead of the claret.

Root vegetables are cheap and nutritious, and when combined with chicken, they make a tasty and economical casserole.

Braised Chicken *with* Dumplings

SERVES 4

4 chicken quarters
2 tbsp sunflower oil
2 leeks, sliced
250 g/9 oz carrots, chopped
250 g/9 oz parsnips, chopped
2 small turnips, chopped
600 ml/1 pint chicken stock
3 tbsp Worcestershire sauce
2 sprigs of fresh rosemary
salt and pepper

dumplings
200 g/7 oz self-raising flour
100 g/3½ oz shredded suet
1 tbsp chopped fresh rosemary leaves
cold water, to mix

1 Remove the skin from the chicken, if preferred. Heat the oil in a large, flameproof casserole or heavy-based saucepan and fry the chicken until golden. Using a slotted spoon, remove the chicken from the pan. Drain off the excess fat.

2 Add the leeks, carrots, parsnips and turnips to the casserole and cook for 5 minutes, until lightly coloured. Return the chicken to the pan.

3 Add the chicken stock, Worcestershire sauce and rosemary, and season with salt and pepper to taste, then bring to the boil.

4 Reduce the heat, cover and simmer gently for about 50 minutes, or until the juices run clear when the chicken is pierced in the thickest part with a skewer.

5 To make the dumplings, combine the flour, suet and rosemary leaves with seasoning in a bowl. Stir in just enough cold water to bind to a firm dough.

6 Form into 8 small balls and place on top of the chicken and vegetables. Cover and simmer for a further 10–12 minutes, until the dumplings are well risen. Serve with the casserole.

NUTRITION
Calories *773*; Sugars *14 g*; Protein *46 g*;
Carbohydrate *59 g*; Fat *41 g*; Saturates *15 g*

 moderate

 25 mins

1 hr 30 mins

This recipe has an Oriental flavour, thanks to the aromatic sesame oil and fresh ginger.

Oriental Chicken *and* Ginger Sauce

1 Heat the oil in a large, heavy-based frying pan. Coat the chicken in the seasoned flour and cook for about 4 minutes, until browned all over. Transfer to a large casserole and keep warm until required.

2 Slowly fry the shallots and mushrooms in the juices.

3 Add the chicken stock, Worcestershire sauce, honey and ginger, then season with salt and pepper to taste.

4 Pour the mixture over the chicken, and cover the casserole with a lid or cooking foil.

5 Cook in the centre of a preheated oven, 150°C/300°F/Gas Mark 2, for about 1½ hours, until the meat is very tender. Add the yogurt and cook for a further 10 minutes. Serve the casserole with a mixture of wild rice and white rice, and garnish with parsley.

SERVES 6 – 8

6 tbsp sesame oil
900 g/2 lb chicken meat, cut into bite-sized
   pieces
55 g/2 oz flour, seasoned
32 shallots, sliced
500 g/1 lb 2 oz wild mushrooms, chopped
   roughly
300 ml/10 fl oz chicken stock
2 tbsp Worcestershire sauce
1 tbsp honey
2 tbsp grated fresh root ginger
salt and pepper
150 ml/5 fl oz natural yogurt
sprigs of fresh flat-leaved parsley, to garnish
wild rice and white rice, to serve

NUTRITION
Calories 277; Sugars 6 g; Protein 28 g;
Carbohydrate 17 g; Fat 11 g; Saturates 2 g

  moderate
  15 mins
  1 hr 50 mins

🍳 **COOK'S TIP**

Mushrooms can be stored in the refrigerator for 24–36 hours. Keep them in paper bags as they 'sweat' in plastic. You do not need to peel them but wild mushrooms must be washed thoroughly.

A tasty way to make chicken joints go a long way. This hearty casserole, spiced with the warm, subtle flavour of ginger, is a good choice for a Halloween party.

Caribbean Chicken Hotpot

SERVES 4

2 tsp sunflower oil
4 chicken drumsticks
4 chicken thighs
1 onion, sliced thinly
750 g/1 lb 10 oz piece squash
    or pumpkin, diced
1 green pepper, deseeded and sliced
2.5-cm/1-inch piece of fresh root ginger,
    chopped finely
400 g/14 oz canned chopped tomatoes
300 ml/10 fl oz chicken stock
55 g/2 oz split red lentils
garlic salt
cayenne pepper
350 g/12 oz canned sweetcorn, drained
salt and pepper
crusty bread, to serve

1 Heat the oil in a large flameproof casserole and fry the chicken joints until golden, turning frequently.

2 Drain any excess fat from the pan and add the onion, squash and green pepper. Gently fry for a few minutes until lightly browned. Add the ginger, tomatoes, chicken stock and lentils. Season lightly with garlic salt and cayenne pepper.

3 Cover the casserole and place in a preheated oven, 190°C/375°F/ Gas Mark 5, for about 1 hour, until the vegetables are tender and the juices run clear when the chicken is pierced through the thickest part with a skewer.

4 Add the sweetcorn and cook for a further 5 minutes. Season with salt and pepper to taste and serve with crusty bread.

NUTRITION
Calories 277; Sugars 6 g; Protein 33 g;
Carbohydrate 22 g; Fat 7 g; Saturates 1 g

⭐⭐   easy
🕐   10 mins
🕐   1 hr 15 mins

 COOK'S TIP

If squash or pumpkin is not available, swede makes a good substitute.

This is a cassoulet with a twist – it is made with chicken instead of duck and lamb. Save time by using canned beans, such as borlotti or cannellini, which are both good in this dish.

Chicken Cassoulet

1 Heat the sunflower oil in an ovenproof casserole and fry the chicken until browned all over. Remove the chicken from the casserole with a slotted spoon and set aside until required.

2 Add the mushrooms, shallots and garlic to the casserole and cook for 4 minutes.

3 Return the chicken to the casserole and sprinkle with the flour, then cook for a further 2 minutes.

4 Add the white wine and chicken stock, stir until boiling, then add the bouquet garni. Season with salt and pepper to taste.

5 Add the beans to the casserole.

6 Cover and place in the centre of a preheated oven, 150°C/ 300°F/ Gas Mark 2, for 2 hours. Remove the bouquet garni and serve the casserole with the steamed squash.

SERVES 4

4 tbsp sunflower oil
900 g/2 lb chicken meat, chopped
250 g/9 oz mushrooms, sliced
16 shallots
6 garlic cloves, crushed
1 tbsp plain flour
250 ml/9 fl oz white wine
250 ml/9 fl oz chicken stock
1 fresh bouquet garni with sage and 1 celery stick
salt and pepper
400 g/14 oz canned borlotti beans, drained and rinsed
steamed squash, to serve

NUTRITION
Calories *550*; Sugars *2 g*; Protein *60 g*;
Carbohydrate *26 g*; Fat *19 g*; Saturates *4 g*

 easy

10 mins

2 hrs 15 mins

🍳 COOK'S TIP

Mushrooms are ideal in a low-fat diet because they are high in flavour and contain no fat. Experiment with the wealth of varieties that are now available from supermarkets.

CHICKEN

This is a slow-cooked, old-fashioned stew to warm you up on a cold winter's day. The rarebit toasts are a perfect accompaniment to soak up the rich juices, but if preferred, serve the stew with jacket potatoes.

Traditional Chicken Stew

SERVES 4 – 6

4 large, skinless chicken thighs
2 tbsp plain flour
2 tbsp mustard powder
2 tbsp sunflower oil
15 g/½ oz butter
4 small onions, cut into wedges
600 ml/1 pint beer
2 tbsp Worcestershire sauce
3 tbsp chopped fresh sage leaves
salt and pepper

to serve
French beans
new potatoes

rarebit toasts
55 g/2 oz mature Cheddar cheese, grated
1 tsp mustard powder
1 tsp plain flour
1 tsp Worcestershire sauce
1 tbsp beer
2 slices wholemeal toast

NUTRITION
Calories *476*; Sugars *30 g*; Protein *56 g*;
Carbohydrate *41 g*; Fat *16 g*; Saturates *5 g*

moderate

25 mins

1 hr 45 mins

1 Toss the chicken in the flour and mustard powder to coat evenly. Heat the sunflower oil and butter in a large, flameproof casserole and fry the chicken over a fairly high heat, turning occasionally, until golden. Remove the chicken from the casserole with a slotted spoon and keep hot.

2 Fry the onions until golden. Add the chicken, beer, Worcestershire sauce and sage, and season with salt and pepper to taste, then bring to the boil. Reduce the heat, cover and simmer gently for about 1½ hours, until the chicken is very tender.

3 Meanwhile, make the rarebit toasts. Mix the cheese with the mustard powder, flour, Worcestershire sauce and beer. Spread the mixture over the toast and cook under a hot grill for about 1 minute, until melted and golden. Cut the toasts into triangles.

4 Serve the stew with the rarebit toasts, French beans and new potatoes.

COOK'S TIP

If you do not have fresh sage, use 2 teaspoons of dried sage in step 2.

A hearty, one-dish meal that would make a substantial lunch or supper. As it requires a long cooking time, make double the quantity and freeze half for later use.

Chicken *and* Bean Casserole

1 Cook the beans in salted boiling water for about 25 minutes.

2 Heat the butter and olive oil in a flameproof casserole, add the bacon and chicken and cook for 5 minutes.

3 Sprinkle with the flour, then add the cider and chicken stock, stirring constantly to prevent lumps forming. Season with salt and pepper to taste and bring to the boil.

4 Add the beans, then cover the casserole tightly with a lid or cooking foil and bake in the centre of a preheated oven, 160°C/325°F/ Gas Mark 3, for 2 hours.

5 About 15 minutes before the end of cooking time, remove the lid or cooking foil from the casserole.

6 In a frying pan, cook the shallots and honey together for 5 minutes, turning the shallots frequently.

7 Add the shallots and cooked beetroot to the casserole and leave to finish cooking in the oven for the last 15 minutes.

SERVES 6

500 g/1 lb 2 oz dried beans, such as flageolet, soaked overnight and drained
25 g/1 oz butter
2 tbsp olive oil
3 rindless bacon rashers, chopped
900 g/2 lb chicken pieces
1 tbsp plain flour
300 ml/10 fl oz cider
150 ml/5 fl oz chicken stock
14 shallots
2 tbsp clear honey, warmed
250 g/8 oz ready-cooked beetroot
salt and pepper

NUTRITION
Calories *529*; Sugars *30 g*; Protein *56 g*; Carbohydrate *41 g*; Fat *16 g*; Saturates *5 g*

 moderate

 24 hrs 15 mins

3 hrs 15 mins

👨‍🍳 **COOK'S TIP**

To save time, use canned flageolet beans instead of dried. Drain and rinse before adding to the chicken.

A colourful casserole packed with sunshine flavours from the Mediterranean. Sun-dried tomatoes add a wonderful richness and you need very few to make this a really special dish.

Rich Chicken Casserole

SERVES 4

8 chicken thighs
2 tbsp olive oil
1 red onion, sliced
2 garlic cloves, crushed
1 large red pepper, deseeded and
   sliced thickly
finely grated rind and juice of 1 small orange
125 ml/4 fl oz chicken stock
400 g/14 oz canned chopped tomatoes
25 g/1 oz sun-dried tomatoes, sliced thinly
1 tbsp chopped fresh thyme
50 g/1¾ oz stoned black olives
salt and pepper
crusty fresh bread, to serve

to garnish
sprigs of fresh thyme
orange rind

1 In a large, heavy-based frying pan, dry-fry the chicken over a fairly high heat, turning occasionally, until golden brown. Using a slotted spoon, drain off any excess fat from the chicken and transfer to a flameproof casserole.

2 Fry the onion, garlic and red pepper in the pan over a moderate heat for 3–4 minutes. Transfer to the casserole.

3 Add the orange rind and juice, chicken stock, tomatoes and sun-dried tomatoes, stir to combine, then bring to the boil.

4 Reduce the heat, cover and simmer over a low heat for about 1 hour, stirring occasionally. Add the chopped thyme and black olives, then season with salt and pepper to taste.

5 Sprinkle the orange rind and thyme over the casserole to garnish, and serve with crusty bread.

NUTRITION
Calories *260*; Sugars *8 g*; Protein *32 g*;
Carbohydrate *8 g*; Fat *11 g*; Saturates *2 g*

 moderate
 15 mins
1 hr 15 mins

🍳 **COOK'S TIP**

Sun-dried tomatoes have a dense texture and concentrated taste, and add intense flavour to slow-cooked casseroles.

Madeira is a fortified wine which can be used in both sweet and savoury dishes. Here, it adds a rich, full flavour to the casserole.

Chicken *and* Madeira Casserole

1 Heat the butter in a large, heavy-based frying pan and cook the onions, carrots, bacon and button mushrooms for 3 minutes, stirring frequently. Transfer to a large casserole dish.

2 Add the chicken to the frying pan and cook until browned all over. Transfer to the casserole dish.

3 Add the white wine and cook until the wine has almost completely reduced.

4 Sprinkle with the seasoned flour, stirring to prevent any lumps forming.

5 Add the chicken stock and bouquet garni, and season with salt and pepper to taste. Cover and cook the casserole for 2 hours. About 30 minutes before the end of the cooking time, add the Madeira and continue to cook uncovered. Remove the bouquet garni.

6 Carve the chicken and serve with the mashed potato.

SERVES 8

25 g/1 oz butter
20 baby onions
250 g/9 oz carrots, sliced
250 g/9 oz bacon, chopped
250 g/9 oz button mushrooms
1 chicken, weighing about 1.5 kg/
  3 lb 5 oz
450 ml/15 fl oz white wine
25 g/1 oz flour, seasoned
450 ml/15 fl oz chicken stock
bouquet garni, fresh or dried
150 ml/5 fl oz Madeira
salt and pepper
mashed potato or pasta, to serve

 COOK'S TIP

You can add any combination of herbs to this recipe – chervil is a popular herb in French cuisine, but add it at the end of cooking so that its delicate flavour is not lost. Other herbs which work well with chicken are parsley and tarragon.

 moderate

25 mins

2 hrs 40 mins

If you have the time, it is preferable to bone the chicken completely, or use skinless chicken breasts.

Californian Chicken

SERVES 6

175 g/6 oz plain flour
1 tsp paprika
1 tsp dried Italian seasoning
1 tsp dried tarragon
1 tsp dried rosemary
2 eggs, beaten
120 ml/4 fl oz milk
1 chicken, weighing about 1.8 kg/4 lb, jointed
flour, seasoned
150 ml/5 fl oz rapeseed oil
2 bananas, quartered
1 eating apple, cored and cut into rings
350 g/12 oz canned sweetcorn and peppers, drained
mixed salad, to serve

NUTRITION
Calories *623*; Sugars *13 g*; Protein *45 g*; Carbohydrate *41 g*; Fat *32 g*; Saturates *4 g*

 moderate

 30 mins

30 mins

55 mins

1 Mix together the flour, spices, herbs and a pinch of salt in a large bowl. Make a well in the centre and add the eggs.

2 Blend well and slowly add the milk, whisking until very smooth.

3 Toss the chicken pieces in the seasoned flour and dip the chicken pieces into the batter mix.

4 Heat the oil in a large, heavy-based frying pan. Add the chicken and fry for about 3 minutes, or until lightly golden. Remove with a slotted spoon and place the chicken pieces on a non-stick baking tray.

5 Meanwhile, batter the bananas and apple rings and fry for 2 minutes, then remove with a slotted spoon. Toss the sweetcorn in the leftover batter.

6 Drop spoonfuls of the sweetcorn mixture into the oil to make flat fritters . Cook for 4 minutes on each side. Keep warm with the apple and banana fritters.

7 Bake the chicken in a preheated oven, 200°C/400°F/Gas Mark 6, for about 25 minutes, until the chicken is tender and golden brown.

8 Arrange the chicken, sweetcorn fritters and the apple and banana fritters on serving plates. Serve with a mixed salad.

Pork adds a tasty flavour to this dish. If you can't find fresh garden peas, frozen peas are a good substitute.

Chicken *and* Green Pea Casserole

1 Melt the butter in a large, heavy-based frying pan. Add the pork and onions and fry gently for 5 minutes, until lightly browned.

2 Remove the pork and onions from the pan and set aside until required. Add the chicken pieces to the pan and cook until browned all over. Transfer the chicken to an ovenproof casserole.

3 Add the flour to the pan and cook, stirring, until it begins to brown, then slowly blend in the chicken stock.

4 Cook the chicken with the sauce and bouquet garni in a preheated oven, 200°C/400°F/Gas Mark 6, for 35 minutes.

5 Remove the bouquet garni about 10 minutes before the end of the cooking time and add the peas and the reserved pork and onions. Stir until combined. Season with salt and pepper to taste.

6 When cooked, place the chicken pieces on a large platter, surrounded with the pork, peas and onions.

SERVES 4

55 g/2 oz butter
250 g/9 oz lean pork, cut into small cubes
16 small onions or shallots, peeled
1 kg/2 lb 4 oz skinless, boneless chicken pieces
25 g/1 oz plain flour
600 ml/1 pint chicken stock
bouquet garni, fresh or dried
500 g/1 lb 2 oz fresh peas
salt and pepper

NUTRITION
Calories *594*; Sugars *6 g*; Protein *77 g*;
Carbohydrate *20 g*; Fat *25 g*; Saturates *9 g*

 moderate

 15 mins

1 hr 10 mins

This richly flavoured stuffing is cooked under the breast skin of the chicken to seal in the flavour and to keep the meat moist and succulent during cooking.

Festive Apple Chicken

SERVES 6

1 chicken, weighing about 1.8 kg/4 lb
oil, for brushing
15 g/½ oz butter
1 tbsp redcurrant jelly
salt and pepper
assorted vegetables, to serve

stuffing
15 g/½ oz butter
1 small onion, finely chopped
55 g/2 oz mushrooms, finely chopped
55 g/2 oz smoked ham, finely chopped
25 g/1 oz fresh breadcrumbs
1 tbsp chopped fresh parsley
3 crisp eating apples
1 tbsp lemon juice

NUTRITION
Calories *219*; Sugars *7 g*; Protein *29 g*;
Carbohydrate *9 g*; Fat *8 g*; Saturates *4 g*

moderate

15 mins

2 hrs 15 mins

1 To make the stuffing, melt the butter in a heavy-based frying pan. Add the onion and cook gently, stirring, until softened but not browned. Stir in the mushrooms and cook for 2–3 minutes. Remove from the heat and stir in the ham, breadcrumbs and the parsley.

2 Core one of the apples, leaving the skin on, and grate coarsely. Add the apple and lemon juice to the stuffing mixture. Season with salt and pepper.

3 Loosen the breast skin of the chicken and carefully spoon the stuffing mixture under it, smoothing the skin over evenly with your hands.

4 Place the chicken in a roasting tin and brush lightly with oil.

5 Roast the chicken in a preheated oven, 190°C/375°F/Gas Mark 5, for 25 minutes per 500 g/1 lb, plus 25 minutes, or until there is no trace of pink in the juices when the chicken is pierced through the thickest part with a skewer. If the breast starts to brown too much, cover the chicken with foil.

6 Core and slice the remaining apples and sauté in the butter until golden. Stir in the redcurrant jelly and warm through until melted. Serve the chicken with the apple slices and with the mixed vegetables.

This recipe for chicken is coated with a fresh-flavoured marinade, then roasted. Serve it with new potatoes and salad.

Coriander Chicken

1 Place the coriander, garlic, salt, pepper, lemon juice and olive oil in a pestle and mortar and pound together or blend in a food processor. Chill for 4 hours to allow the flavours to develop.

2 Place the chicken in a roasting tin. Coat generously with the coriander and garlic mixture.

3 Sprinkle with more pepper and roast in a preheated oven, 190°C/375°F/Gas Mark 5, on a low shelf for 1½ hours, basting every 20 minutes with the coriander mixture. If the chicken starts to brown, cover with foil. Carve the chicken, garnish with parsley and serve with potatoes and carrots.

SERVES 4 – 6

3 sprigs of fresh coriander, chopped
4 garlic cloves
½ tsp salt
1 tsp pepper
4 tbsp lemon juice
4 tbsp olive oil
1 chicken, weighing about 2.25 kg/5 lb
sprigs of fresh parsley, to garnish

to serve
new potatoes
carrot batons

NUTRITION
Calories *404*; Sugars *0 g*; Protein *47 g*; Carbohydrate *1 g*; Fat *24 g*; Saturates *5 g*

COOK'S TIP

When grinding up small quantities, using a pestle and mortar instead of a food processor will save wasting any of the mixture.

moderate

4 hrs 10 mins

1 hr 30 mins

Chicken goes well with most savoury herbs. This combination makes a good partner for tangy feta cheese and a rich tomato sauce.

Feta Chicken *with* Mountain Herbs

SERVES 4

8 skinless, boneless chicken thighs
2 tbsp each of chopped fresh thyme,
    rosemary and oregano
125 g/4½ oz feta cheese, cut into 8 sticks
1 tbsp milk
2 tbsp plain flour
salt and pepper
sprigs of fresh thyme, rosemary and
    oregano, to garnish
sugar snap peas, to serve

tomato sauce
1 onion, roughly chopped
1 garlic clove, crushed
1 tbsp olive oil
4 plum tomatoes, quartered
sprig each of fresh thyme, rosemary
    and oregano

NUTRITION
Calories *318*; Sugars *6 g*; Protein *28 g*;
Carbohydrate *15 g*; Fat *17 g*; Saturates *7 g*

easy

25 mins

1 hr

1 Spread out the chicken thighs on a board, smooth side downwards.

2 Divide the herbs between the chicken thighs, then place one stick of cheese in the centre of each chicken thigh. Season with salt and pepper to taste, then roll up each chicken thigh to enclose the cheese.

3 Place the rolls in an ovenproof dish, brush with milk and dust with flour to coat evenly.

4 Bake in a preheated oven, 190°C/375°F/Gas Mark 5, for 25–30 minutes, or until golden brown and the juices should run clear, not pink, when the chicken is pierced in the thickest part with a skewer.

5 To make the sauce, cook the onion and garlic in the olive oil, stirring, until softened and beginning to brown.

6 Add the tomatoes, reduce the heat, cover and simmer gently for 15–20 minutes, until soft.

7 Add the herbs, then transfer to a food processor and blend to a purée. Press through a sieve to make a smooth, rich sauce. Season to taste. Garnish the chicken with herbs and serve with the sauce and sugar snap peas.

Poussins (young chickens) are ideal for one or two people, and can be cooked very easily and quickly for a special dinner. If you're preparing this for one, a microwave makes it even quicker and more convenient.

Poussins *with* Dried Fruit

1 Place the dried fruit in a bowl, cover with the boiling water and leave to stand for about 30 minutes.

2 Cut the chickens in half down the breastbone using a sharp knife, or leave them whole, if preferred.

3 Mix the fruit and any juices remaining in the bowl with the walnut halves, honey and ground allspice and divide the mixture between 2 small roasting bags or squares of foil.

4 Brush the chickens with the walnut oil and season with salt and pepper to taste, then place them on top of the fruit.

5 Close the roasting bags or fold the foil over to enclose the chickens and bake on a baking tray in a preheated oven, 190°C/375°F/Gas Mark 5, for 25–30 minutes, until the juices run clear, not pink, when the chicken is pierced in the thickest part with a skewer. (To cook in a microwave, use microwave roasting bags and cook on High power for 6–7 minutes each, depending on their size.)

6 Serve with fresh vegetables and new potatoes.

COOK'S TIP

Alternative dried fruit that can be used in this recipe include cherries, mangoes or pawpaws.

SERVES 2

125 g/4½ oz ready-to-eat dried apples, peaches and prunes
120 ml/4 fl oz boiling water
2 poussins
25 g/1 oz walnut halves
1 tbsp honey
1 tsp ground allspice
1 tbsp walnut oil
salt and pepper

to serve
fresh vegetables
new potatoes

NUTRITION
Calories *316*; Sugars *23 g*; Protein *23 g*; Carbohydrate *23 g*; Fat *15 g*; Saturates *2 g*

 easy
 40 mins
40 mins
30 mins

CHICKEN

Marmalade lovers will enjoy this festive recipe. You can use any favourite marmalade, including lemon or grapefruit.

Chicken *with* Marmalade Sauce

SERVES 6

1 chicken, weighing about 2.25 kg/5 lb
bay leaves

stuffing
1 celery stick, chopped finely
1 small onion, chopped finely
1 tbsp sunflower oil, plus extra for brushing
125 g/4½ oz fresh wholemeal breadcrumbs
4 tbsp marmalade
2 tbsp chopped fresh parsley
1 egg, beaten
salt and pepper

sauce
2 tsp cornflour
2 tbsp orange juice
3 tbsp marmalade
150 ml/5 fl oz chicken stock
1 orange, peeled and segmented
2 tbsp brandy

NUTRITION
Calories *436*; Sugars *20 g*; Protein *45 g*;
Carbohydrate *30 g*; Fat *15 g*; Saturates *4 g*

  moderate
  25 mins
  2 hrs 10 mins

1 Lift the neck flap of the chicken and remove the wishbone using a small, sharp knife. Place a sprig of bay leaves inside the body cavity.

2 For the stuffing, sauté the celery and onion in the oil until softened. Add the breadcrumbs, 3 tablespoons of the marmalade, parsley and egg. Season with salt and pepper to taste and use to stuff the neck cavity of the chicken. Any extra stuffing can be cooked separately.

3 Place the chicken in a roasting tin and brush lightly with oil. Roast in a preheated oven, 190°C/375°F/ Gas Mark 5, for 20 minutes per 500 g/1 lb 2 oz, plus 20 minutes, or until the juices run clear when the chicken is pierced in the thickest part with a skewer. Remove from the oven and glaze with the remaining marmalade.

4 Meanwhile, make the sauce. Blend the cornflour with the orange juice in a pan, then add the marmalade and chicken stock. Heat gently, stirring, until thickened and smooth. Remove from the heat. Just before serving, add the orange segments and brandy to the sauce and bring to the boil.

5 Serve the chicken with the orange sauce, any extra stuffing and new potatoes.

This dish, which uses a partly-boned chicken is easy to slice and serve. If preferred, stuff the bird in the traditional way, then cook any remaining stuffing separately.

Glazed Cranberry Chicken

1 To part-bone the chicken, dislocate the legs and place the chicken breast-side downwards. Cut a straight line through the skin along the ridge of the back. Scrape the meat down from the bone on both sides.

2 When you reach the point where the legs and wings join the body, cut through the joints. Work around the ribcage until the carcass can be lifted away.

3 For the stuffing, mix the mango with the cranberries, breadcrumbs and mace, then bind with the egg. Season with salt and pepper to taste.

4 Place the chicken skin-side down in a roasting tin. Spoon half of the stuffing over. Arrange the bacon rolls down the centre then top with the remaining stuffing. Fold the skin over and tie with string. Turn the chicken over, truss the legs and tuck the wings underneath. Mix together the turmeric, honey and oil and brush the mixture over the skin.

5 Roast in a preheated oven, 190°C/375°F/Gas Mark 5, for 1½–2 hours, until the juices run clear, not pink, when the chicken is pierced in the thickest part with a skewer. When the chicken starts to brown, cover loosely with foil to prevent it over-browning. Serve the chicken with seasonal vegetables.

SERVES 4

1 chicken, weighing about 2.25 kg/5 lb
6 rashers smoked bacon, each rolled up
½ tsp ground turmeric
2 tsp honey
2 tsp sunflower oil
salt and pepper
seasonal vegetables, to serve

stuffing

1 ripe mango, stoned and diced
55g/2 oz fresh or frozen cranberries
125 g/4½ oz fresh breadcrumbs
½ tsp ground mace
1 egg, beaten

NUTRITION
Calories *629*; Sugars *10 g*; Protein *61 g*;
Carbohydrate *33 g*; Fat *29 g*; Saturates *8 g*

✪✪✪✪ challenging

 40 mins

 1 hr 30 mins

CHICKEN

Chicken suprêmes have a little bit of the wing bone remaining. In this recipe, a tart, fruity sauce perfectly complements the bird.

Chicken *with* Bacon *and* Redcurrants

SERVES **8**

55 g/2 oz butter
juice of 1 lemon
250 g/9 oz redcurrants or cranberries
1–2 tbsp muscovado sugar
8 skinless chicken suprêmes or breasts
16 rashers of streaky bacon
1 tbsp chopped fresh thyme
55 g/2 oz beef dripping
4 slices of bread, cut into triangles
salt and pepper

1 Heat the butter in a heavy-based saucepan. Add the lemon juice, redcurrants and muscovado sugar and season with salt and pepper to taste. Cook for 1 minute and allow to cool until required.

2 Meanwhile, season the chicken. Wrap 2 slices of streaky bacon around each breast and sprinkle with thyme.

3 Wrap each breast in a piece of lightly greased foil and place in a roasting tin. Roast in a preheated oven, 200°C/400°F/Gas Mark 6, for 15 minutes. Remove the foil and roast for a further 10 minutes.

4 Heat the dripping in a frying pan, add the bread triangles and fry on both sides until golden brown.

5 Arrange the chicken breasts with the triangles on a large serving plate. Serve with a spoonful of the fruit sauce.

NUTRITION
Calories *458*; Sugars *7 g*; Protein *42 g*;
Carbohydrate *16 g*; Fat *26 g*; Saturates *12 g*

⭐⭐⭐   moderate
🕐   15 mins
🕐   35 mins

👨‍🍳 COOK'S TIP

You can use either fresh thyme or dried thyme in this recipe, but remember that dried herbs have a stronger flavour so you need half the quantity.

The Catalan region of Spain is famous for its wonderful combinations of meat with fruit. Here, peaches lend a touch of sweetness, while the pine nuts, cinnamon and sherry add an unusual twist.

Spanish Chicken *with* Peaches

1 Combine the breadcrumbs with 25 g/1 oz of the pine nuts, egg and thyme.

2 Remove the skin of the peaches, if liked. Dice 1 peach into small pieces and stir into the breadcrumb mixture. Season with salt and pepper to taste. Spoon the stuffing into the neck cavity of the chicken, securing the skin firmly over it.

3 Place the chicken in a roasting tin. Sprinkle the cinnamon over the skin.

4 Cover loosely with foil and roast in a preheated oven, 190°C/375°F/Gas Mark 5, for 1 hour, basting occasionally.

5 Remove the foil and spoon the sherry over the chicken. Cook for a further 30 minutes, basting with the sherry, until the juices run clear, not pink, when the chicken is pierced in the thickest part with a skewer.

6 Sprinkle the rest of the pine nuts over the remaining peach halves and place in an ovenproof dish in the oven for the final 10 minutes of the cooking time.

7 Lift the chicken on to a serving plate and arrange the peach halves around it. Skim any fat from the juices, stir in the cream and heat gently. Serve the sauce with the chicken.

SERVES **6**

55 g/2 oz fresh brown breadcrumbs
55 g/2 oz pine nuts
1 small egg, beaten
4 tbsp chopped fresh thyme or 1 tbsp dried thyme
4 fresh peaches, halved and stoned or 8 canned peach halves
1 chicken, weighing about 2.5 kg/5 lb 8 oz
1 tsp ground cinnamon
200 ml/7 fl oz amontillado sherry
4 tbsp double cream
salt and pepper

NUTRITION
Calories *586*; Sugars *9 g*; Protein *46 g*;
Carbohydrate *14 g*; Fat *36 g*; Saturates *14 g*

 moderate

 25 mins

1 hr 30 mins

This recipe is rather time-consuming but it is well worth the effort. Cherries and chicken make a good flavour combination.

Suprême *of* Chicken *with* Cherries

SERVES 6

6 large chicken suprêmes
6 black peppercorns, crushed
300 g/10½ oz stoned black cherries, or canned stoned cherries
12 shallots, sliced
4 rashers rindless, streaky bacon, chopped
8 juniper berries
4 tbsp port
150 ml/5 fl oz red wine
25 g/1 oz butter
2 tbsp walnut oil
25 g/1 oz flour
salt and pepper

to serve
new potatoes
French beans

NUTRITION
Calories *363*; Sugars *10 g*; Protein *40 g*;
Carbohydrate *14 g*; Fat *14 g*; Saturates *5 g*

 moderate
 48 hrs 15 mins
1 hr

1 Place the chicken in an ovenproof dish. Add the peppercorns, cherries and the shallots. Add the bacon, juniper berries, port and red wine, stir well to combine. Season with salt and pepper to taste.

2 Place the chicken in the refrigerator and leave to marinate for 48 hours.

3 Heat the butter and walnut oil in a large, heavy-based frying pan. Remove the chicken from the marinade and fry quickly in the pan for 4 minutes on each side.

4 Return the chicken to the marinade, reserving the butter, oil and juices in the pan.

5 Cover the chicken with foil and bake in a preheated oven, 180°C/350°F/ Gas Mark 4, for 20 minutes. Transfer the chicken from the baking tin to a warm serving dish. Add the flour to the juices in the frying pan and cook for 4 minutes, add the marinade and bring to the boil. Reduce the heat and simmer for 10 minutes, until the sauce becomes smooth.

6 Pour the cherry sauce over the chicken suprêmes and serve with new potatoes and French beans.

An unusual change from a plain roast, with a distinctly warming Scottish flavour and a delicious oatmeal stuffing.

Whisky Roast Chicken

1 To make the stuffing, fry the onion and celery in the butter, stirring over a moderate heat until softened and lightly browned.

2 Remove from the heat and stir in the thyme, oats and stock, and season with salt and pepper to taste.

3 Stuff the neck end of the chicken with the mixture and tuck the neck flap under. Place in a roasting tin, brush lightly with oil, and roast in a preheated oven, 190°C/375°F/Gas Mark 5, for about 1 hour.

4 Mix the heather honey with 1 tablespoon of the whisky and brush the mixture over the chicken. Return to the oven for a further 20 minutes, or until golden brown and the juices run clear, not pink, when the chicken is pierced through the thickest part with a skewer.

5 Lift the chicken on to a serving plate. Skim the fat from the juices then stir in the flour. Stir over a moderate heat until the mixture starts to bubble, then gradually add the stock and remaining whisky, then bring to the boil.

6 Reduce the heat and simmer, stirring, for 1 minute and serve the chicken with the sauce, broccoli and sautéed potatoes.

SERVES 6

4 tbsp chicken stock
salt and pepper
1 chicken, weighing about 2 kg/4 lb 8 oz
oil, for brushing
1 tbsp heather honey
2 tbsp Scotch whisky
2 tbsp plain flour

stuffing
1 onion, chopped finely
1 stick celery, sliced thinly
25 g/1 oz butter or 1 tbsp sunflower oil
1 tsp dried thyme
4 tbsp porridge oats
300 ml/10 fl oz chicken stock
salt and pepper

to serve
broccoli
sautéed potatoes

NUTRITION
Calories 254; Sugars 6 g; Protein 27 g; Carbohydrate 11 g; Fat 8 g; Saturates 2 g

✪✪✪ moderate

 5 mins

 1 hr 30 mins

CHICKEN

This delicious chicken dish has the flavour of roast chicken but unusually it is finished off in a casserole and served with a wild mushroom sauce.

Roast Chicken *with* Wild Mushrooms

SERVES 4

85 g/3 oz butter, softened
1 garlic clove, crushed
1 chicken, weighing about 2 kg/4 lb 8 oz
175 g/6 oz wild mushrooms
12 shallots
25 g/1 oz plain flour
150 ml/5 fl oz brandy
300 ml/10 fl oz double cream
salt and pepper
1 tbsp chopped fresh parsley, to garnish

to serve
roast potatoes
French beans

NUTRITION
Calories *920*; Sugars *4 g*; Protein *50 g*;
Carbohydrate *10 g*; Fat *68 g*; Saturates *38 g*

 moderate

 2 hrs 25 mins

2 hrs

1 Place the butter and garlic in a bowl. Season with salt and pepper to taste and combine well.

2 Rub the mixture inside and outside of the chicken and leave for 2 hours.

3 Place the chicken in a large roasting tin and roast in the centre of a preheated oven, 230°C/450°F/ Gas Mark 8, for 1½ hours, basting with the garlic butter every 10 minutes.

4 Remove the chicken from the roasting tin and set aside to cool slightly.

5 Transfer the chicken juices to a saucepan and cook the mushrooms and shallots for 5 minutes. Sprinkle with the flour. Add the warm brandy and ignite using a taper or long match.

6 Add the double cream and cook for 3 minutes on a very low heat, stirring all the time.

7 Bone the chicken and cut into small bite-sized pieces, then place the meat in a casserole dish.

8 Cover the chicken with the mushroom sauce and cook in the oven, with the heat reduced to 160°C/325°F/Gas Mark 3, for a further 12 minutes. Garnish with the parsley and serve with roast potatoes and French beans.

This low-fat recipe is great for summer entertaining, served simply with a green salad and new potatoes. If you spatchcock the chicken (cut it in half and press it flat) you can roast it in under an hour.

Honeyed Citrus Chicken

1 Put the chicken on a chopping board with the breast downwards. Cut through the bottom part of the carcass using poultry shears or heavy kitchen scissors, making sure not to cut right through to the breast bone.

2 Rinse the chicken with cold water, drain and place on a board with the skin side uppermost. Press the chicken flat, then cut off the leg ends.

3 Thread 2 long wooden skewers through the bird to keep it flat. Season the skin with salt and pepper to taste.

4 Put all the marinade ingredients, except the orange wedges, in a shallow, non-metallic dish. Mix, add the chicken, then cover and chill for 4 hours, turning occasionally.

5 To make the sauce, mix all the ingredients together and season. Spoon into a serving dish, cover and chill.

6 Transfer the chicken and marinade to a roasting tin, open out the chicken and place skin-side downwards. Tuck the orange wedges around the chicken and roast in a preheated oven, 200°C/400°F/Gas Mark 6, for 25 minutes. Turn the chicken over and roast for a further 20–30 minutes.

7 Baste until the chicken has browned and the juices run clear, not pink, when pierced in the thickest part with a skewer. Garnish with tarragon and serve with the citrus sauce.

SERVES 4

1 chicken, weighing about 2 kg/4 lb 8 oz
2 oranges, cut into wedges
salt and pepper

marinade
300 ml/10 fl oz orange juice
3 tbsp cider vinegar
3 tbsp clear honey
2 tbsp chopped fresh tarragon

sauce
handful of fresh tarragon sprigs, chopped, plus extra to garnish
200 g/7 oz fat-free fromage frais
2 tbsp orange juice
1 tsp clear honey
55 g/2 oz stuffed olives, chopped

NUTRITION
Calories *288*; Sugars *32 g*; Protein *30 g*; Carbohydrate *32 g*; Fat *6 g*; Saturates *1 g*

✪✪✪✪ challenging
 4 hrs 20 mins
  55 mins

Beetroot is one of the most underrated vegetables, adding flavour and colour to numerous dishes. Tender young beetroot are used in this recipe.

Breast *of* Chicken *with* York Ham

SERVES 4

4 chicken suprêmes
8 fresh sage leaves
8 thin slices of York ham
250 g/9 oz Stilton cheese, cut into 8 slices
8 slices rindless streaky bacon
150 ml/5 fl oz chicken stock
2 tbsp port
24 shallots
500 g/1 lb 2 oz baby beetroot, cooked
1 tbsp cornflour, blended with a little port
salt and pepper

1 Cut a long slit horizontally along each chicken suprême to make a pocket.

2 Insert 2 sage leaves into each pocket and season with salt and pepper to taste.

3 Wrap each slice of ham around a slice of cheese and place 2 into each chicken pocket. Carefully wrap enough bacon around each breast to completely cover the pockets containing the ham and the cheese.

4 Place the breasts in an ovenproof casserole dish and add the stock and Port.

5 Add the shallots, cover with a lid or cooking foil and braise in a preheated oven, 190°C/375°F/ Gas Mark 5, for about 40 minutes.

6 Carefully place each suprême on to a cutting board and slice through them to create a fan effect. Arrange on a warm serving dish with the shallots and beetroot.

7 Put the juices from the casserole into a saucepan and bring to the boil, remove from the heat and add the cornflour paste. Reduce the heat and simmer the sauce for 2 minutes, then pour it over the shallots and beetroot before serving.

NUTRITION
Calories 529; Sugars 30 g; Protein 56 g;
Carbohydrate 41 g; Fat 16 g; Saturates 5 g

 moderate

 25 mins

25 mins

45 mins

COOK'S TIP

Use any blue-veined cheese, such as Gorgonzola or Roquefort, instead of the Stilton, if preferred.

Poussins are simple to prepare, and take about 30 minutes to roast. One chicken makes a substantial serving for each person.

Poussins *with* Herbs *and* Wine

1 In a bowl, mix together the breadcrumbs, one-third of the fromage frais and 2 tablespoons each of parsley and chives. Season with salt and pepper to taste, then spoon the mixture into the neck ends of the chickens. Place the chickens on a rack in a roasting tin, brush with oil and season well.

2 Roast in a preheated oven, 220°C/425°F/Gas Mark 7, for 30–35 minutes, until the juices run clear, not pink, when the chickens are pierced in the thickest part with a skewer.

3 Place the vegetables in a shallow, ovenproof dish in one layer and add half the remaining herbs with the chicken stock. Cover and bake for 25–30 minutes, until tender. Strain the vegetables, reserving the cooking juices, and keep warm.

4 Lift the chickens on to a serving plate and skim any fat from the juices in the tin. Add the reserved vegetable juices.

5 Blend the cornflour with the wine and whisk into the sauce with the remaining fromage frais. Whisk until boiling, then add the remaining herbs. Season to taste. Spoon the sauce over the chickens and serve with the vegetables.

SERVES 4

5 tbsp fresh brown breadcrumbs
200 g/7 oz fromage frais or low-fat crème fraîche
5 tbsp chopped fresh parsley
5 tbsp chopped fresh chives
4 poussins (young chickens)
1 tbsp sunflower oil
salt and pepper
675 g/1½ lbs young spring vegetables, such as carrots, courgettes, sugar snap peas, sweetcorn and turnips, cut into small chunks
120 ml/4 fl oz boiling chicken stock
2 tsp cornflour
150 ml/5 fl oz dry white wine

NUTRITION
Calories *280*; Sugars *7 g*; Protein *32 g*; Carbohydrate *16 g*; Fat *7 g*; Saturates *2 g*

 moderate

20 mins

 1 hr 15 mins

It's relatively easy to bone a whole chicken, but you can ask a friendly butcher to do this for you, if preferred.

Garlic Chicken *with* Mortadella

SERVES 6

1 chicken, weighing about 2.25 kg/5 lb
8 slices mortadella or salami
125 g/4½ oz fresh white or brown breadcrumbs
125 g/4½ oz Parmesan cheese, grated
2 garlic cloves, crushed
6 tbsp chopped fresh basil or parsley
1 egg, beaten
olive oil, for brushing
pepper
fresh vegetables, to serve

1 Bone the chicken, keeping the skin intact. Dislocate each leg by breaking it at the thigh joint. Cut down each side of the backbone, taking care not to pierce the breast skin.

2 Pull the backbone clear of the flesh and discard. Remove the ribs, severing any attached flesh with a sharp knife.

3 Scrape the flesh from each leg and cut away the bone at the joint with a knife or shears.

4 Use the bones for stock. Lay out the boned chicken on a board, skin-side down. Arrange the mortadella slices over the chicken, overlapping slightly.

5 Put the breadcrumbs, Parmesan, garlic and basil in a bowl. Season with pepper to taste and mix well. Stir in the beaten egg to bind the mixture together. Pile the mixture down the middle of the boned chicken, roll the meat around it and tie securely with fine cotton string.

6 Place in a roasting dish and brush lightly with olive oil. Roast in a preheated oven, 200°C/400°F/Gas Mark 6, for 1½ hours, or until the juices run clear, not pink, when the chicken is pierced in the thickest part with a skewer.

7 Serve hot or cold, in slices, with the vegetables.

NUTRITION
Calories 578; Sugars 0.4 g; Protein 42 g;
Carbohydrate 9 g; Fat 42 g; Saturates 15 g

✪✪✪✪ challenging

🕐 35 mins

🕐 1 hr 30 mins

A cheesy stuffing is tucked under the breast skin of the chicken to give added flavour and moistness to the meat.

Chicken *with* Lime Stuffing

1 To make the stuffing, trim and coarsely grate 85 g/3 oz of the courgettes and mix with the cheese, lime rind and breadcrumbs, and season with salt and pepper to taste.

2 Carefully ease the skin away from the breast of the chicken.

3 Push the stuffing under the chicken skin with your fingers, to cover the breast evenly.

4 Place the chicken in a roasting tin, brush with oil and roast in a preheated oven, 190°C/375°F/Gas Mark 5, for 20 minutes per 500 g/1 lb 2 oz, plus 20 minutes, or until the juices run clear, not pink, when the thickest part of the chicken is pierced with a skewer.

5 Meanwhile, trim the remaining courgettes and cut into long, thin strips with a potato peeler or sharp knife. Sauté in the butter and lime juice until just tender, then serve with the chicken.

SERVES 6

340 g/12 oz courgettes
85 g/3 oz medium-fat soft cheese
finely grated rind and juice of 1 lime
2 tbsp fresh breadcrumbs
1 chicken, weighing about 2.25 kg/5 lb
oil, for brushing
25 g/1 oz butter
salt and pepper

NUTRITION
Calories *236*; Sugars *1 g*; Protein *28 g*;
Carbohydrate *3 g*; Fat *12 g*; Saturates *7 g*

 moderate
 15 mins
2 hrs

COOK'S TIP

Finely grate the courgettes, rather than cutting them into strips, to reduce the cooking time.

This colourful, nutritious pot roast makes an ideal family meal or special dinner. Add more vegetables if you're feeding a crowd.

Pot Roast Orange Chicken

SERVES 4

2 tbsp sunflower oil
1 chicken, weighing about 1.5 kg/3 lb 5 oz
2 large oranges
2 small onions, quartered
500 g/1 lb 2 oz small whole carrots or thin carrots, cut into 5-cm/2-inch lengths
150 ml/5 fl oz orange juice
2 tbsp brandy
2 tbsp sesame seeds
1 tbsp cornflour
salt and pepper

1 Heat the oil in a large flameproof casserole and fry the chicken, turning occasionally until evenly browned.

2 Cut one orange in half and place half inside the chicken cavity. Place the chicken in a large, deep casserole. Arrange the onions and carrots around the chicken. Season with salt and pepper to taste and add the orange juice.

3 Cut the remaining oranges into thin wedges and tuck around the chicken, among the vegetables.

4 Cover and cook in a preheated oven, 180°C/350°F/Gas Mark 4, for about 1½ hours, or until the juices run clear, not pink, when the chicken is pierced, in the thickest part with a skewer and the vegetables are tender. Remove the lid and sprinkle with the brandy and sesame seeds, and return to the oven for 10 minutes.

5 To serve, lift the chicken on to a large platter. Place the vegetables around the chicken. Skim any excess fat from the juices. Blend the cornflour with 1 tablespoon cold water, then stir into the juices and bring to the boil, stirring. Adjust the seasoning, then serve the sauce with the chicken.

NUTRITION
Calories 302; Sugars 17 g; Protein 29 g; Carbohydrate 22 g; Fat 11 g; Saturates 2 g

 moderate

 10 mins

2 hrs

🍴 **COOK'S TIP**

Use lemons instead of oranges for a sharper citrus flavour and place a sprig of fresh thyme in the chicken cavity with the lemon half.

Chicken portions are brushed with a classic combination of honey and mustard, then coated in crunchy poppy seeds.

Honey *and* Mustard-baked Chicken

1 Place the chicken pieces, skinless-side down, on a large baking tray.

2 Place all the ingredients, except the poppy seeds, into a large bowl and blend together thoroughly. Brush the mixture over the chicken portions.

3 Bake in the centre of a preheated oven, 200°C/400°F/Gas Mark 6, for 15 minutes.

4 Carefully turn the chicken pieces over and coat the top with the remaining honey and mustard mixture.

5 Sprinkle the chicken with poppy seeds and return to the oven for a further 15 minutes.

6 Arrange the chicken on a serving dish, pour over the cooking juices and serve with a tomato and sweetcorn salad.

SERVES 4 – 6

8 chicken portions
55 g/2 oz butter, melted
4 tbsp mild mustard
4 tbsp clear honey
2 tbsp lemon juice
1 tsp paprika
3 tbsp poppy seeds
salt and pepper
tomato and sweetcorn salad, to serve

NUTRITION

Calories *464*; Sugars *17 g*; Protein *64 g*; Carbohydrate *18 g*; Fat *20 g*; Saturates *10 g*

 easy

 15 mins

30 mins

🍳 COOK'S TIP

Mexican rice makes an excellent accompaniment to this dish: boil the rice in vegetable stock with fresh chilli and vegetables, including onions, tomatoes, garlic, carrots and peas.

A roast that is full of Mediterranean flavour. A mixture of feta cheese, rosemary and sun-dried tomatoes is stuffed under the chicken skin.

Mediterranean Roast Chicken

SERVES 6

1 chicken, weighing about 2.5 kg/5 lb 8 oz
3 sprigs of fresh rosemary, chopped
175 g/6 oz feta cheese, grated coarsely
2 tbsp sun-dried tomato paste
55 g/2 oz butter, softened
1 bulb garlic
1 kg/2 lb 4 oz new potatoes, halved if large
1 each red, green and yellow pepper,
   deseeded and cut into chunks
3 courgettes, sliced thinly
2 tbsp olive oil
2 tbsp plain flour
600 ml/1 pint chicken stock
salt and pepper

NUTRITION

Calories *488*; Sugars *6 g*; Protein *37 g*;
Carbohydrate *34 g*; Fat *23 g*; Saturates *11 g*

 moderate

 35 mins

  2 hrs

1 Carefully cut between the chicken skin and the top of the breast meat using a small pointed knife. Slide a finger into the slit and carefully enlarge it to form a pocket. Continue until the skin is completely lifted away from both breasts and the top of the legs.

2 Mix the rosemary with the feta, sun-dried tomato paste and butter and season with pepper to taste, then spoon the mixture under the skin. Put the chicken in a large roasting tin, cover with foil and cook in a preheated oven, 190°C/375°F/Gas Mark 5, for 20 minutes per 500 g/1 lb 2 oz, plus 20 minutes.

3 Break the garlic bulb into cloves but do not peel. Add the vegetables to the chicken after 40 minutes.

4 Drizzle with oil, tuck in a few sprigs of rosemary and season well. Cook for the remaining time, removing the foil for the last 40 minutes to brown the top of the chicken.

5 Transfer the chicken to a serving platter. Place some of the vegetables around the chicken and transfer the remainder to a warm serving dish. Spoon any fat from the roasting tin and stir the flour into the remaining pan juices. Cook for 2 minutes, then gradually stir in the stock. Bring to the boil, stirring until thickened. Strain into a sauce boat and serve with the chicken.

Cheese and mustard make a simple, crisp coating for this quick and healthy dish.

Cheddar-baked Chicken

1 Mix together the milk and mustard in a bowl. In another bowl, combine the cheese, flour and chives.

2 Dip the chicken into the milk and mustard mixture, brushing to coat evenly.

3 Dip the chicken breasts into the cheese mixture, pressing to coat evenly. Place on a baking tray and spoon any spare cheese coating over the top.

4 Bake in a preheated oven, 200°C/400°F/Gas Mark 6, for 30–35 minutes, until golden brown and the juices run clear, not pink, when the chicken is pierced in the thickest part with a skewer. Serve the chicken with a jacket potato and crisp salad.

SERVES 4

1 tbsp milk
2 tbsp prepared English mustard
55 g/2 oz mature Cheddar cheese, grated
3 tbsp plain flour
2 tbsp chopped fresh chives
4 skinless, boneless chicken breasts

to serve
jacket potatoes
crisp salad

NUTRITION
Calories 225; Sugars 1 g; Protein 32 g;
Carbohydrate 9 g; Fat 7 g; Saturates 3 g

 very easy

10 mins

 35 mins

🍳 **COOK'S TIP**

There are several varieties of mustard available. For a sharper flavour, try French varieties – Meaux mustard has a grainy texture with a warm, spicy flavour, while Dijon mustard is medium-hot and tangy.

CHICKEN

Any combination of small, young vegetables can be roasted with the chicken, including courgettes, leeks and onions.

Gardener's Chicken

SERVES 4

1 chicken, weighing about 1.5 kg/3 lb 5 oz
bunch of fresh parsley
½ onion
25 g/1 oz butter, softened
4 tbsp olive oil
500 g/1 lb 2 oz new potatoes
500 g/1 lb 2 oz baby carrots
salt and pepper
chopped fresh parsley, to garnish

stuffing

250 g/9 oz parsnips, chopped
125 g/4½ oz carrots, chopped
25 g/1 oz fresh breadcrumbs
¼ tsp grated nutmeg
1 tbsp chopped fresh parsley

NUTRITION
Calories *674*; Sugars *18 g*; Protein *35 g*;
Carbohydrate *45 g*; Fat *40 g*; Saturates *12 g*

 moderate
 15 mins
1 hr 45 mins

1 To make the stuffing, put the parsnips and carrots into a pan, half cover with water and bring to the boil. Reduce the heat, cover and simmer until tender. Drain well, then purée in a blender or food processor. Transfer the purée to a bowl and leave to cool.

2 Mix in the breadcrumbs, nutmeg and parsley and season with salt and pepper to taste.

3 Put the stuffing into the neck end of the chicken and push a little under the skin over the breast meat. Secure the flap of skin with a small metal skewer or cocktail stick.

4 Place the bunch of parsley and onion inside the cavity of the chicken, then place the chicken in a large roasting tin.

5 Spread the butter over the skin and season, cover with foil and place in a preheated oven, 190°C/375°F/Gas Mark 5, for 30 minutes.

6 Meanwhile, heat the oil in a heavy-based frying pan, and lightly brown the potatoes.

7 Transfer the potatoes to the roasting tin and add the carrots. Baste the chicken and continue to cook for a further 1 hour, basting the chicken and vegetables after 30 minutes. Remove the foil for the last 20 minutes to allow the skin to crisp. Garnish the vegetables with chopped parsley and serve.

Fresh spring vegetables are the basis of this colourful casserole, which is topped with hearty wholemeal dumplings.

Spring-time Chicken Cobbler

1 Heat the oil in a large, heavy-based frying pan and fry the chicken, turning occasionally, until golden brown. Drain well and place in a casserole. Add the onion to the pan and cook, stirring occasionally, for 2–3 minutes, until softened.

2 Add the carrots and turnips to the casserole with the onions and beans.

3 Blend the cornflour with a little of the stock, then stir in the rest and heat gently, stirring until boiling. Pour into the casserole and add the bay leaves. Season with salt and pepper to taste.

4 Cover tightly and bake in a preheated oven, 200°C/ 400°F/Gas Mark 6, for 50–60 minutes, until the juices run clear, not pink, when the chicken is pierced in the thickest part with a skewer.

5 For the topping, sift the flour and baking powder into a bowl. Mix in the margarine with a fork. Stir in the mustard, cheese and enough milk to make a fairly soft dough.

6 Roll out and cut 16 rounds with a 4-cm/1½-inch cutter. Uncover the casserole, arrange the scone rounds on top of the chicken, then brush with milk and sprinkle with sesame seeds. Return to the oven and bake for 20 minutes, or until the topping is golden and firm.

SERVES 4

1 tbsp vegetable oil
8 skinless chicken drumsticks
1 small onion, sliced
350 g/12 oz baby carrots, cut into bite-sized pieces
2 baby turnips, cut into bite-sized pieces
125 g/4½ oz broad beans or peas
1 tsp cornflour
300ml/10 fl oz chicken stock
2 bay leaves
salt and pepper

cobbler topping
250 g/9 oz plain wholemeal flour
2 tsp baking powder
2 tbsp soft sunflower margarine
2 tsp dry wholegrain mustard
55 g/2 oz low-fat mature Cheddar cheese, grated
skimmed milk, to mix, plus extra for brushing
sesame seeds, for sprinkling

NUTRITION
Calories *560*; Sugars *10 g*; Protein *389 g*; Carbohydrate *64 g*; Fat *18 g*; Saturates *4 g*

moderate

15 mins

1 hr 30 mins

Barbecues *and* Grills

There is nothing more delicious than the juicy flesh and charred skin of a chicken that has been grilled over an open fire, after marinating in a flavoursome mixture of oil and herbs or spices. Try an Asian-style mixture of yogurt and aromatic spices, or soy sauce, sesame oil and fresh root ginger. There are some unusual flavours and innovative tastes, including Chicken Kebabs with Blackberry Sauce, and Mediterranean Chicken Kebabs, which are attractive whirls of chicken, bacon and basil. Poussins, flavoured with lemon and tarragon, are perfect for grilling or barbecuing. There is also a recipe for Mint Chicken with Mixed Vegetables, which combines chicken breasts with a selection of grilled vegetables, including courgettes, aubergine and red pepper drizzled with olive oil and served with crusty bread to soak up the delicious juices.

These spicy chicken wings are good served with a chilli salsa and salad. Alternatively, if this is too spicy for you, try a soured cream and chive dip.

Chicken Cajun-style

SERVES 4

16 chicken wings
4 tsp paprika
2 tsp ground coriander
1 tsp celery salt
1 tsp ground cumin
½ tsp cayenne pepper
½ tsp salt
1 tbsp oil
2 tbsp red wine vinegar
fresh parsley, to garnish

to serve
cherry tomatoes
mixed salad leaves
sauce, such as chilli salsa or soured cream
    and chive dip

1 Remove the wing tips of the chicken with kitchen scissors.

2 Mix together the paprika, ground coriander, celery salt, ground cumin, cayenne pepper, salt, oil and red wine vinegar.

3 Rub this mixture over the wings to coat evenly and set aside in the refrigerator for at least 1 hour to allow the flavours to permeate the chicken.

4 Cook the chicken wings on a preheated barbecue, occasionally brushing with oil, for about 15 minutes, turning often until cooked through.

5 Garnish the chicken with fresh parsley and serve with cherry tomatoes, mixed salad leaves and a sauce of your choice.

NUTRITION
Calories *430*; Sugars *13 g*; Protein *40 g*;
Carbohydrate *7 g*; Fat *6 g*; Saturates *2 g*

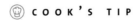

  very easy

  1 hr 10 mins

  15 mins

🍳 **COOK'S TIP**

To save time, you can buy ready-made Cajun spice seasoning to rub over the chicken wings.

This is a quick and easy recipe for the grill, perfect for lunch or to eat outdoors on a picnic. The chicken tastes good both hot or cold.

Spicy Sesame Chicken

1 Make cuts in the chicken flesh at intervals with a sharp knife.

2 In a bowl, combine the natural yogurt, lemon rind and juice and curry paste to form a smooth mixture.

3 Spoon the mixture over the chicken and arrange on a foil-lined grill pan or baking tray.

4 Place the chicken quarters under a preheated medium-hot grill and cook for 12–15 minutes, turning once. Grill until golden brown and thoroughly cooked. Just before the end of the cooking time, sprinkle the chicken with the sesame seeds.

5 Serve with a salad, naan bread and lemon wedges.

SERVES 4

4 chicken quarters
150 g/5½ oz natural yogurt
finely grated rind and juice of 1 small lemon
2 tsp medium-hot curry paste
1 tbsp sesame seeds

to serve
salad
naan bread
lemon wedges

NUTRITION
Calories *110*; Sugars *3 g*; Protein *15 g*;
Carbohydrate *3 g*; Fat *4 g*; Saturates *1 g*

 very easy

5 mins

15 mins

COOK'S TIP
Poppy seeds, fennel seeds or cumin seeds, or a mixture of all three, can also be used to sprinkle over the chicken.

CHICKEN

Chicken wings and corn in a sticky ginger marinade are best eaten with the fingers – there's no other way!

Ginger Chicken *and* Corn

SERVES 6

3 corn-on-the-cobs, each cut into 6 slices
12 chicken wings
2.5-cm/1-inch piece of fresh root ginger, grated or chopped finely
6 tbsp lemon juice
4 tsp sunflower oil
1 tbsp golden caster sugar

to serve
jacket potatoes
mixed salad

1 Place the corn-on-the-cob slices in a large bowl with the chicken wings.

2 Mix the ginger with the lemon juice, sunflower oil and golden caster sugar, then toss with the sweetcorn and chicken to coat.

3 Thread the sweetcorn and chicken wings on to metal or presoaked wooden skewers, to make turning easier.

4 Cook the sweetcorn and chicken under a preheated medium-hot grill or barbecue for 15–20 minutes, basting with the ginger glaze. Turn frequently until the sweetcorn is golden brown and tender and the chicken is cooked. Serve with jacket potatoes and salad.

NUTRITION
Calories *123*; Sugars *3 g*; Protein *14 g*;
Carbohydrate *3 g*; Fat *6 g*; Saturates *1 g*

 very easy
 10 mins
 20 mins

COOK'S TIP

Cut off the wing tips before grilling as they burn very easily. Alternatively, you can cover them with small pieces of foil.

Grilling is a quick and healthy method of cooking, ideal for sealing in the juices and flavour of chicken breasts, and a wonderful way to cook summer vegetables.

Mint Chicken *with* Mixed Vegetables

1 Place the aubergine slices in a colander and sprinkle with salt. Leave over a bowl to drain for 30 minutes, then rinse and dry. This will get rid of any bitter juices.

2 Mix together the garlic, lemon rind, mint and olive oil and season with salt and pepper to taste.

3 Slash the chicken breasts at intervals with a sharp knife. Spoon over about half of the oil mixture over the chicken and stir to combine.

4 Combine the aubergines and the remaining vegetables, then toss in the rest of the oil mixture. Marinate the chicken and vegetables for about 30 minutes.

5 Cook the chicken breasts and vegetables on a preheated hot grill or barbecue, turning occasionally, until they are golden brown and tender, or cook on a ridged griddle pan on the hob.

6 Brush the bread slices with olive oil and grill until golden.

7 Drizzle a little olive oil over the chicken and grilled vegetables and serve hot or cold with the toasted bread slices.

SERVES 4

1 small aubergine, sliced
2 garlic cloves, crushed
finely grated rind of ½ lemon
1 tbsp chopped fresh mint
6 tbsp olive oil, plus extra for brushing
4 skinless, boneless chicken breasts
2 courgettes, sliced
1 red pepper, deseeded and quartered
1 small bulb fennel, sliced thickly
1 large red onion, sliced thickly
1 small ciabatta loaf or 1 French baguette, sliced
salt

NUTRITION
Calories *611*; Sugars *11 g*; Protein *43 g*;
Carbohydrate *66 g*; Fat *21 g*; Saturates *3 g*

★★★   moderate
    1 hr 5 mins
    25 mins

CHICKEN

In this recipe, chicken kebabs are given a Caribbean flavour. The marinade keeps them moist and succulent during cooking.

Tropical Chicken Skewers

SERVES 6

750 g/1 lb 10 oz skinless, boneless chicken breasts, cut into 2.5-cm/1-inch cubes
2 tbsp medium sherry
3 mangoes, stoned and cut into 2.5-cm/1-inch cubes
bay leaves
2 tbsp oil
2 tbsp coarsely shredded coconut
pepper
crisp salad, to serve

1 Toss the chicken in the sherry, and season with a little pepper.

2 Thread the chicken, mango and bay leaves alternately on to metal or pre-soaked wooden skewers, then brush lightly with oil.

3 Grill the skewers on a preheated moderately hot grill for about 8–10 minutes, turning occasionally, until golden.

4 Sprinkle the skewers with the coconut and grill for a further 30 seconds. Serve with a crisp salad.

NUTRITION

Calories 225; Sugars 11 g; Protein 31 g; Carbohydrate 11 g; Fat 6 g; Saturates 2 g

 easy

 20 mins

10 mins

🍳 COOK'S TIP

Use mangoes that are ripe but still firm so that they hold together on the skewers during cooking. Pineapple is a suitable alternative to the mango.

Chicken drumsticks are marinated to impart a tangy, sweet-and-sour flavour and a shiny glaze.

Sweet *and* Sour Drumsticks

1 Skin the chicken, if desired, and slash 2–3 times with a sharp knife.

2 Lay the chicken drumsticks side by side in a shallow, non-metallic container.

3 Mix the red wine vinegar, tomato purée, soy sauce, honey, Worcestershire sauce, garlic and cayenne pepper together and pour the mixture over the chicken drumsticks.

4 Leave to marinate in the refrigerator for 1 hour. Cook the drumsticks on a preheated barbecue for about 20 minutes, brushing with the marinade and turning during cooking. Garnish with parsley and serve with a crisp salad.

SERVES 4

8 chicken drumsticks
4 tbsp red wine vinegar
2 tbsp tomato purée
2 tbsp soy sauce
2 tbsp clear honey
1 tbsp Worcestershire sauce
1 garlic clove
good pinch of cayenne pepper
sprigs of fresh parsley, to garnish
crisp salad, to serve

NUTRITION
Calories *171*; Sugars *9 g*; Protein *23 g*; Carbohydrate *10 g*; Fat *5 g*; Saturates *1 g*

 COOK'S TIP

For a tangy flavour, add the juice of 1 lime to the marinade. While the drumsticks are grilling, check regularly to ensure that they are not burning.

 very easy
 1 hr 15 mins
 20 mins

CHICKEN

Warm weather calls for lighter eating, and this chilled chicken dish in a subtle herb vinaigrette is ideal for a summer dinner party or picnic.

Chicken *with* Garden Herbs

SERVES 4

4 skinless, part-boned chicken breasts
6 tbsp olive oil
2 tbsp lemon juice
4 tbsp finely chopped summer herbs,
    such as parsley, chives and mint
1 ripe avocado, stoned
125 g/4½ oz low-fat fromage frais
pepper

to serve
cold rice
fresh red chillies, sliced
spring onions, sliced

1 Using a sharp knife, cut 3–4 deep slashes in the chicken breasts.

2 Place the chicken breasts in a flameproof dish and brush lightly with a little of the olive oil.

3 Cook the chicken under a preheated medium-hot grill, turning once, until golden and the juices run clear, not pink, when the chicken is pierced in the thickest part with a skewer.

4 Combine the remaining oil with the lemon juice and herbs and season with pepper to taste. Spoon the oil over the chicken and leave to cool. Chill in the refrigerator for at least 1 hour.

5 Mash the avocado or purée in a food processor with the fromage frais. Season with pepper to taste. Serve the chicken with the avocado sauce and cold rice, sprinkled with chillies and spring onions.

NUTRITION
Calories 370; Sugars 3 g; Protein 33 g;
Carbohydrate 3 g; Fat 25 g; Saturates 4 g

 easy

1 hr 15 mins

25 mins

🍳 **COOK'S TIP**

To remove the stone easily from an avocado, first cut it in half. Holding one half securely in your hand, rap the knife into the stone so that it becomes embedded in the stone, then carefully twist the knife to dislodge the stone.

These low-fat, spicy skewers are cooked in a matter of minutes. They can be assembled ahead of time and stored in the refrigerator until needed.

Skewered Spicy Tomato Chicken

1 Place the chicken in a bowl. Mix together the tomato purée, honey, Worcestershire sauce and rosemary. Add to the chicken, stirring to coat evenly.

2 Thread the chicken pieces and tomatoes alternately on to 8 presoaked wooden skewers.

3 Spoon any remaining glaze over. Cook under a preheated hot grill for 8–10 minutes, turning occasionally, until the chicken is thoroughly cooked. Serve garnished with sprigs of rosemary on a bed of couscous.

SERVES 4

500 g/1 lb 2 oz skinless, boneless chicken breasts, cut into 2.5-cm/1-inch cubes
3 tbsp tomato purée
2 tbsp clear honey
2 tbsp Worcestershire sauce
1 tbsp chopped fresh rosemary
250 g/9 oz cherry tomatoes
sprigs of fresh rosemary, to garnish
couscous or rice, to serve

NUTRITION
Calories *195*; Sugars *11 g*; Protein *28 g*;
Carbohydrate *12 g*; Fat *4 g*; Saturates *1 g*

very easy

10 mins

10 mins

 COOK'S TIP

Cherry tomatoes are ideal for barbecues as they can be threaded straight on to skewers. As they are kept whole, the skins retain the natural juices.

This Italian-style dish is richly flavoured with pesto, which is a mixture of basil, olive oil, pine nuts and Parmesan cheese. Red or green pesto can be used for this recipe.

Grilled Chicken *with* Pesto Toasts

SERVES 4

8 part-boned chicken thighs
olive oil, for brushing
400 ml/14 fl oz passata
120 ml/4 fl oz green or red pesto sauce
12 slices French bread
85 g/3 oz Parmesan cheese, grated
55 g/2 oz pine nuts or flaked almonds
salad leaves, to serve

1 Arrange the chicken in a single layer in a wide flameproof dish and brush lightly with oil.

2 Cook under a preheated medium-hot grill for about 15 minutes, turning occasionally, until golden brown and the juices run clear, not pink, when the chicken is pierced in the thickest part with a skewer.

3 Pour off any excess fat. Warm the passata and half the pesto sauce in a small saucepan and pour it over the chicken. Grill for a few more minutes, turning until coated.

4 Meanwhile, spread the remaining pesto on to the bread. Sprinkle with the Parmesan cheese and pine nuts. Grill for 2–3 minutes, until browned and bubbling. Serve with a the salad leaves.

NUTRITION
Calories 787; Sugars 6 g; Protein 45 g;
Carbohydrate 70 g; Fat 38 g; Saturates 9 g

 easy

10 mins

25 mins

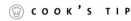 COOK'S TIP

Although leaving the skin on the chicken means that it will have a higher fat content, many people like its rich taste and crispy texture, especially when it is blackened by the barbecue. The skin also seals in the cooking juices.

Great for barbecues, simple summer lunches or picnics, this is an easy and tasty chicken dish.

Mustard Barbecue Drumsticks

1 Chop 2 of the bacon rashers into small pieces and fry without fat for 3–4 minutes, stirring so that the bacon does not stick to the bottom of the pan. Remove from the heat and stir in the garlic, 2 tablespoons of the wholegrain mustard and the breadcrumbs.

2 Carefully loosen the skin from each drumstick with your fingers, being careful not to tear the skin. Spoon a little of the mustard stuffing under each flap of skin, smoothing the skin over firmly afterwards.

3 Wrap a bacon rasher around each drumstick and secure with cocktail sticks.

4 Mix together the remaining mustard and oil, brush it over the chicken drumsticks and cook on a preheated medium-hot barbecue or grill for about 25 minutes, until the juices run clear, not pink, when the chicken is pierced in the thickest part with a skewer.

5 Garnish with the parsley sprigs. The drumsticks may be served hot or cold.

SERVES 4

10 slices smoked streaky bacon
1 garlic clove, crushed
3 tbsp wholegrain mustard
4 tbsp fresh brown breadcrumbs
8 chicken drumsticks
1 tbsp sunflower oil
sprigs of fresh parsley, to garnish

COOK'S TIP

Don't cook the chicken over the hottest part of the barbecue or the outside may be charred before the centre is cooked.

NUTRITION
Calories 394; Sugars 5 g; Protein 40 g;
Carbohydrate 3 g; Fat 27 g; Saturates 8 g

moderate

20 mins

30 mins

These tangy lime and honey-coated pieces have a matching sauce or dip, based on creamy natural yogurt. They could be served at a barbecue or as a main course for a dinner party.

Minty Limed Chicken

SERVES 6

3 tbsp finely chopped fresh mint
4 tbsp clear honey
4 tbsp lime juice
12 boneless chicken thighs
mixed salad, to serve

sauce
150 g/5½ oz thick natural yogurt
1 tbsp finely chopped fresh mint
2 tsp finely grated lime rind

1 Combine the mint, honey and lime juice in a shallow dish.

2 Use cocktail sticks to keep the chicken thighs in neat shapes and add the chicken to the marinade, turning to coat evenly.

3 Leave to marinate for at least 30 minutes, preferably overnight. Cook the chicken on a preheated medium-hot barbecue or grill, turning frequently and basting with the marinade. The chicken is cooked if the juices run clear, not pink, when the chicken is pierced in the thickest part with a skewer.

4 Meanwhile, mix together the sauce ingredients.

5 Remove the cocktail sticks and serve the chicken with a salad and the sauce.

NUTRITION
Calories *170*; Sugars *12 g*; Protein *23 g*;
Carbohydrate *12 g*; Fat *3 g*; Saturates *1 g*

easy

40 mins

20 mins

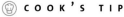 **COOK'S TIP**

Mint can be grown very easily in a garden or window box. It is a useful herb for marinades and salad dressings. Other useful herbs are parsley and basil.

This autumnal recipe can be made with freshly picked wild blackberries from the hedgerow, if you're lucky enough to have a good supply.

Chicken Kebabs *with* Blackberry Sauce

1 Place the chicken in a bowl with the white wine and rosemary, and season with pepper to taste. Cover and leave to marinate in the refrigerator for at least 1 hour.

2 Drain the chicken, reserving the marinade, and thread the meat on to 8 metal or presoaked wooden skewers.

3 Cook on a preheated moderately hot grill for 8–10 minutes, turning occasionally, until golden and evenly cooked.

4 Meanwhile, to make the sauce, place the marinade in a pan with the blackberries and simmer gently until soft. Press the mixture though a sieve using the back of a spoon.

5 Return the blackberry purée to the pan with the cider vinegar and redcurrant jelly and bring to the boil. Boil, uncovered, until the sauce has reduced by about one-third.

6 Place the chicken skewers on serving plates and drizzle the blackberry sauce over the top. Sprinkle with nutmeg and serve with salad, garnished with rosemary and blackberries.

SERVES 4

4 skinless, boneless chicken breasts or 8 thighs, cut into 2.5-cm/1-inch cubes
4 tbsp dry white wine or cider
2 tbsp chopped fresh rosemary
pepper
200 g/7 oz blackberries
1 tbsp cider vinegar
2 tbsp redcurrant jelly
¼ tsp grated nutmeg
pepper
green salad, to serve

to garnish
sprigs of fresh rosemary
blackberries

COOK'S TIP

If you use canned fruit, omit the redcurrant jelly.

NUTRITION

Calories *174*; Sugars *5 g*; Protein *27 g*; Carbohydrate *5 g*; Fat *4 g*; Saturates *1 g*

 easy

 1 hr 15 mins

20 mins

Spatchcocked young chickens are complemented here by the delicate fragrance of lemon and tarragon.

Tarragon Poussins *with* Lemon

SERVES 2

2 poussins (young chickens)
4 sprigs of fresh tarragon, plus extra to garnish
1 tsp oil
25 g/1 oz butter
rind of ½ lemon
1 tbsp lemon juice
1 garlic clove, crushed
salt and pepper
new potatoes, to serve
lemon slices, to garnish

1 Prepare the chickens: turn them breast-side down on a chopping board and cut them through the backbone using kitchen scissors. Crush each bird gently to break the bones so that they lie flat while cooking. Season each with salt.

2 Turn them over and insert a sprig of tarragon under the skin and over each side of the breast.

3 Brush the chickens with oil, using a pastry brush, and place under a preheated hot grill about 13-cm/5-inches from the heat. Grill the chickens for about 15 minutes, turning half way through, until they are lightly browned.

4 Meanwhile, to make the glaze, melt the butter in a small saucepan. Add the lemon rind and juice and garlic. Season with salt and pepper to taste.

5 Brush the baby chickens with the glaze and cook for a further 15 minutes, turning them once and brushing regularly so that they stay moist. Garnish the chickens with tarragon and lemon slices and serve with new potatoes.

NUTRITION
Calories *449*; Sugars *2 g*; Protein *38 g*;
Carbohydrate *5 g*; Fat *30 g*; Saturates *10 g*

moderate

20 mins

35 mins

🍴 **COOK'S TIP**
Once the chickens are flattened, insert 2 metal skewers through them to keep them flat.

Chicken quarters are barbecued, then served with a pungent garlic mayonnaise or aïoli, which originated in Provence in the South of France.

BARBECUES & GRILLS

Chicken *with* Warm Aïoli

1 Using a skewer, prick the chicken quarters in several places, then place in a shallow dish.

2 Combine the oil, lemon juice and thyme and season with salt and pepper to taste. Pour the mixture over the chicken, turning to coat the chicken evenly. Set aside for 2 hours in the refrigerator.

3 To make the aïoli, beat together the garlic and a pinch of salt to make a paste. Add the egg yolks and beat well. Gradually add the oils, drop by drop, beating vigorously, until the mayonnaise becomes creamy and smooth. Add the oils in a thin steady trickle and continue beating until the aïoli has thickened. Stir in the lemon juice and season with pepper. Set aside in a warm place.

4 Place the chicken on a preheated barbecue and cook for 25–30 minutes. Brush with the marinade and turn the portions to cook evenly. Remove and arrange on a serving plate.

5 Beat the water into the aïoli and turn into a warmed serving bowl. Serve the chicken with the aïoli, a green salad and lemon slices.

SERVES 4

4 chicken quarters
2 tbsp oil
2 tbsp lemon juice
2 tsp dried thyme
salt and pepper
green salad, to serve
lemon slices, to garnish

aïoli

5 garlic cloves, crushed
2 egg yolks
120 ml/4 fl oz each olive oil and
    sunflower oil
2 tsp lemon juice
2 tbsp boiling water

NUTRITION
Calories *873*; Sugars *0 g*; Protein *40 g*; Carbohydrate *1 g*; Fat *79 g*; Saturates *12 g*

moderate

2 hrs 35 mins

30 mins

COOK'S TIP

To make a quick aïoli, add the garlic to 300 ml/10 fl oz good-quality mayonnaise, then place in a bowl over a pan of warm water and beat together. Beat in 1–2 tablespoons hot water just before serving.

CHICKEN

These unusual chicken kebabs have a wonderful Mediterranean flavour, and the bacon helps keep them moist during the cooking.

Mediterranean Chicken Kebabs

SERVES 4

4 skinless, boneless chicken breasts
1 garlic clove, crushed
2 tbsp tomato purée
4 rashers smoked back bacon
large handful of fresh basil leaves
salt and pepper
oil, for brushing
green salad, to serve

1 Spread out a piece of chicken between 2 sheets of clingfilm. Beat firmly with a rolling pin to flatten the chicken to an even thickness. Repeat with the remaining pieces of chicken.

2 Mix together the garlic and tomato purée until well blended. Spread the mixture evenly over the surface of the chicken.

3 Lay a bacon rasher over each piece of chicken, then scatter with the fresh basil leaves. Season with salt and pepper to taste.

4 Roll up each piece of chicken firmly, then cut into thick slices using a sharp knife. Thread the slices securely on to 4 presoaked wooden skewers, making sure the skewer holds the chicken in a spiral shape.

5 Brush the skewers lightly with oil and cook on a preheated hot barbecue or grill for about 5 minutes, then turn the skewers over and cook for a further 5 minutes, until the chicken is cooked through. Serve the chicken spirals hot with a green salad.

NUTRITION

Calories *231*; Sugars *1 g*; Protein *29 g*;
Carbohydrate *1 g*; Fat *13 g*; Saturates *5 g*

⭐⭐ easy

🌀 15 mins

🕐 10 mins

 COOK'S TIP

To complete the Mediterranean theme, serve these kebabs with Parmesan-topped garlic bread.

Tomato ketchup is a very useful ingredient in Oriental dishes, as it imparts a zingy sweet-sour flavour.

Filipino Chicken

1 Combine the lemonade, gin, tomato ketchup, garlic salt and Worcestershire sauce in a large non-metallic dish. Season with salt and pepper to taste.

2 Put the chicken into the dish and turn to coat in the marinade.

3 Leave to marinate in the refrigerator for 2 hours. Remove and leave, covered, at room temperature for 30 minutes.

4 Place the chicken over a medium-hot barbecue and cook for 20 minutes. Turn the chicken once, halfway through the cooking time.

5 Remove from the barbecue and leave to rest for 3–4 minutes before serving.

6 Serve with egg noodles, tossed with a little green chilli and spring onions.

SERVES 4

1 can lemonade or lime-and-lemonade
2 tbsp gin
4 tbsp tomato ketchup
2 tsp garlic salt
2 tsp Worcestershire sauce
4 lean chicken suprêmes or breast fillets
salt and pepper

to serve
dried thread egg noodles
1 fresh green chilli, chopped finely
2 spring onions, sliced

NUTRITION
Calories *194*; Sugars *7 g*; Protein *28 g*;
Carbohydrate *8 g*; Fat *4 g*; Saturates *1 g*

 easy

2 hrs 45 mins

20 mins

COOK'S TIP

Cooking the chicken on the bone after it has reached room temperature means that it requires less time to cook, which ensures that it remains moist.

CHICKEN

These succulent chicken kebabs are coated in a sweet lime marinade and are served with a lime and mango salsa. They make an ideal meal.

Lime Chicken Kebabs

SERVES 4

4 skinless, boneless chicken breasts, about 125 g/4½ oz each, sliced thinly
3 tbsp lime marmalade
1 tsp white wine vinegar
½ tsp finely grated lime rind
1 tbsp lime juice
salt and pepper

to serve
lime wedges
plain white rice, sprinkled with chilli powder

salsa
1 small mango, peeled, stoned and diced
1 small red onion, chopped finely
1 tbsp lime juice
1 tbsp chopped fresh coriander

1 Thread the chicken on to 8 presoaked wooden skewers, so that the meat forms an S-shape down each skewer.

2 Mix together the lime marmalade, vinegar, lime rind and juice. Season with salt and pepper to taste.

3 Arrange the chicken kebabs on the grill rack. Brush the lime marinade generously over the chicken and cook under a preheated medium-hot grill for 5 minutes. Turn the chicken over, brush with the marinade again and grill for a further 4–5 minutes, until the chicken is cooked through.

4 Meanwhile, prepare the salsa. Place the mango, onion, lime juice and coriander in a small bowl and mix well. Season, cover and chill until required.

5 Serve the chicken kebabs with the salsa, accompanied with wedges of lime and plain rice sprinkled with chilli powder.

NUTRITION
Calories *199*; Sugars *14 g*; Protein *28 g*;
Carbohydrate *14 g*; Fat *4 g*; Saturates *1 g*

⭐⭐ easy
 15 mins
 10 mins

🍴 **COOK'S TIP**

To prevent sticking, lightly oil the metal skewers or dip the wooden skewers in water before threading on the chicken .

Chicken tikka is a popular, low-fat Indian dish. Recipes can vary but it is best to try your own combination of spices to suit your taste.

Chicken Tikka Kebabs

1 Place the chicken in a shallow dish. Mix together the garlic, ginger, chilli, yogurt, tomato purée and spices, and season with salt and pepper to taste. Spoon the mixture over the chicken, cover and chill for 2 hours.

2 Toss the mango in the lime juice, cover and chill until required.

3 Thread the chicken and mango pieces alternately on to 8 metal or presoaked wooden skewers. Place the skewers on a grill rack and brush the chicken with the yogurt marinade and the lime juice left from the mango.

4 Place under a preheated medium-hot grill for 6–7 minutes. Turn over, brush again with the marinade and lime juice and cook for a further 6–7 minutes, until cooked and tender.

5 Serve on a bed of rice on a warm platter, garnished with coriander and accompanied by lime wedges, salad and naan bread.

SERVES 4

4 skinless, boneless chicken breasts, about 125 g/4½ oz each, cut into 2.5-cm/ 1-inch cubes
1 garlic clove, crushed
1 tsp grated fresh root ginger
1 fresh green chilli, deseeded and chopped finely
6 tbsp low-fat natural yogurt
1 tbsp tomato purée
1 tsp ground cumin
1 tsp ground coriander
1 tsp ground turmeric
1 large, ripe mango, peeled, stoned and cubed
1 tbsp lime juice
salt and pepper
sprigs of fresh coriander, to garnish

to serve
plain white rice
lime wedges
mixed salad
warm naan bread

NUTRITION
Calories *191*; Sugars *8 g*; Protein *30 g*; Carbohydrate *8 g*; Fat *4 g*; Saturates *2 g*

easy

2 hrs 15 mins

15 mins

CHICKEN

You can use any chicken portions for this recipe. Thighs are economical for large barbecue parties, but you could also use wings or drumsticks.

Sweet Maple Chicken

SERVES 4

12 skinless, boneless chicken thighs
5 tbsp maple syrup
1 tbsp caster sugar
grated rind and juice of ½ orange
2 tbsp tomato ketchup
2 tsp Worcestershire sauce

to garnish
orange slices
sprigs of fresh parsley

to serve
Italian bread, such as focaccia
salad leaves
cherry tomatoes, quartered

1 Using a long sharp knife, make 2–3 diagonal slashes in the flesh of the chicken to allow the flavours of the marinade to permeate. Arrange the chicken thighs in a single layer in a shallow, non-metallic dish.

2 To make the marinade, combine the maple syrup, sugar, orange rind and juice, tomato ketchup and Worcestershire sauce in a small bowl.

3 Pour the marinade over the chicken, turning the chicken to coat thoroughly. Cover with clingfilm and chill in the refrigerator until required.

4 Remove the chicken from the marinade, reserving the marinade.

5 Transfer the chicken to the barbecue and cook over hot coals for 20 minutes, turning the chicken and basting frequently with the marinade. (Alternatively, cook under a preheated medium-hot grill for 20 minutes, turning and basting.)

6 Transfer the chicken to warm serving plates and garnish with slices of orange and sprigs of parsley. Serve immediately with Italian bread, fresh salad leaves and cherry tomatoes.

NUTRITION

Calories *122*; Sugars *16 g*; Protein *11 g*;
Carbohydrate *17 g*; Fat *1 g*; Saturates *1 g*

  moderate

35 mins

20 mins

The chicken is marinated in an aromatic sauce before being barbecued. Use bay leaves, if kaffir lime leaves are unavailable.

Thai-style Chicken Skewers

1 To make the marinade, place the red curry paste in a small saucepan and cook over a medium heat for 1 minute. Add half of the coconut milk to the pan and bring the mixture to the boil. Boil for 2–3 minutes, until the liquid has reduced by about two-thirds.

2 Remove the pan from the heat and stir in the remaining coconut milk. Set aside to cool.

3 Stir the chicken into the cold marinade, cover and chill in the refrigerator for at least 2 hours.

4 Remove the chicken pieces from the marinade and thread them on to skewers, alternating the chicken with the vegetables and lime leaves.

5 Combine the oil and lime juice in a small bowl and brush the mixture over the kebabs. Barbecue the skewers over hot coals, turning and basting frequently for 10–15 minutes, until the chicken is cooked through. Barbecue the tomato halves for the last few minutes of the cooking time and serve with the chicken skewers.

SERVES 4

4 skinless, boneless chicken breasts, cut into 2.5-cm/1-inch cubes
1 onion, cut into wedges
1 large red pepper, deseeded and cut into 2.5-cm/1-inch pieces
1 large yellow pepper, deseeded and cut into 2.5-cm/1-inch pieces
12 kaffir lime leaves
2 tbsp sunflower oil
2 tbsp lime juice
tomato halves, to serve

marinade
1 tbsp Thai red curry paste
150 ml/5 fl oz canned coconut milk

NUTRITION
Calories *218*; Sugars *4 g*; Protein *28 g*; Carbohydrate *5 g*; Fat *10 g*; Saturates *2 g*

easy
2 hrs 15 mins
20 mins

COOK'S TIP

Cooking the marinade first intensifies the flavour. It is important to allow the marinade to cool before adding the chicken because any bacteria may breed in the warm temperature.

143

人

CHICKEN

This is a barbecue variation of the traditional dish, Chicken Maryland. Serve with corn-on-the-cob.

Maryland Chicken Kebabs

SERVES 4

1 tbsp white wine vinegar
1 tbsp lemon juice, plus extra for brushing
1 tbsp golden syrup or clear honey
6 tbsp olive oil
1 garlic clove, crushed
8 skinless, boneless chicken thighs, cut into bite-sized pieces
4 slices rindless, smoked, streaky bacon
2 bananas, cut into 2.5-cm/1-inch pieces
salt and pepper

to serve
4 corn-on-the-cob
mango chutney

1 Combine the white wine vinegar, lemon juice, syrup or honey, oil and garlic in a large bowl. Season with salt and pepper to taste. Add the chicken to the marinade and toss until it is well coated. Cover and set aside to marinate for 1–2 hours.

2 Stretch the bacon rashers with the back of a knife and cut each one in half. Brush the bananas with lemon juice to prevent them from turning brown. Wrap a piece of bacon around each piece of banana.

3 Remove the chicken from the marinade, reserving the marinade for basting. Thread the chicken pieces and the bacon and banana rolls alternately on to metal or pre-soaked wooden skewers.

4 Barbecue the kebabs over hot coals for 8–10 minutes, until the chicken is completely cooked through. Baste the kebabs with the marinade and turn the skewers frequently.

5 Serve with corn-on-the-cob and mango chutney.

NUTRITION
Calories *443*; Sugars *14 g*; Protein *37 g*; Carbohydrate *16 g*; Fat *26 g*; Saturates *6 g*

moderate

2 hrs 30 mins

10 mins

🍴 **COOK'S TIP**

For a quick Maryland-style dish, omit the marinating and cook the chicken thighs over hot coals for about 20 minutes, basting with the marinade. Barbecue the bananas in their skins beside the chicken.

Economical and flavoursome, these tasty chicken liver skewers make an ideal light lunch or a perfect addition to a summer brunch party.

Sherried Liver Brochettes

1 To make the marinade, combine the sherry, oil and mustard in a shallow dish. Season with salt and pepper to taste . Add the chicken livers to the marinade and toss until well coated. Set aside to marinate for 3–4 hours.

2 To make the mayonnaise, stir the mustard into the mayonnaise and chill in the refrigerator.

3 Stretch the bacon with the back of a knife and cut each slice in half. Remove the chicken livers from the marinade, reserving the marinade for basting. Wrap the bacon around half of the chicken liver pieces. Thread the bacon and chicken liver rolls and the plain chicken liver pieces alternately on to 6 presoaked wooden skewers.

4 Barbecue the skewers over hot coals for about 10-12 minutes, turning and frequently basting with the reserved marinade.

5 Meanwhile, cut the bread into 6 pieces and toast the cut sides on the barbecue until golden brown.

6 To serve, top the toasted bread with spinach leaves and place the brochettes on top. Spoon over the mustard mayonnaise and serve immediately.

SERVES **4**

400 g/14 oz chicken livers, trimmed, cleaned and cut into 5-cm/2-inch pieces
3 rashers rindless, streaky bacon
1 ciabatta loaf or small French stick
225 g/8 oz baby spinach leaves

marinade
150 ml/5 fl oz dry sherry
4 tbsp olive oil
1 tsp wholegrain mustard
salt and pepper

mustard mayonnaise
8 tbsp mayonnaise
1 tsp wholegrain mustard

NUTRITION
Calories *767*; Sugars *3 g*; Protein *31 g*;
Carbohydrate *51 g*; Fat *43 g*; Saturates *8 g*

✪✪✪   moderate

🕐   4 hrs 30 mins

🕐   15 mins

Spicy Dishes

Since chicken is so popular throughout the world, there are countless spicy recipes from Asia, Mexico, the Caribbean, Spain and Japan. Lime juice, peanuts, coconut and chilli add the authentic tastes of Thailand to Chilli Coconut Chicken, while Kashmiri Chicken is a rich and spicy dish from Northern India with an aromatic sauce made from yogurt, tikka curry paste, cumin, ginger, chilli and almonds. From Spain comes Spanish Chicken with Prawns with its unusual mixture of chicken and shellfish, together with the famous spicy Spanish sausage, chorizo, slow-cooked in a sauce of garlic, tomatoes and white wine. Lemon and Apricot Chicken is a creative modern dish that would be perfect for any special occasion. There is even a dish from Japan, Teppanyaki, a simple dish of fried chicken with peppers, spring onions and beansprouts, served with a mirin dipping sauce.

This tasty chicken dish combines warm spices, including star anise, ginger and ground coriander. Serve it with plain rice.

Warm Spiced Chicken *with* Almonds

SERVES 4

25 g/1 oz butter
90 ml/3 fl oz vegetable oil
4 skinless, boneless chicken breasts, cut into
   4 x 2-cm/2 x 1-inch pieces
1 onion, chopped roughly
2-cm/1-inch piece of fresh root ginger
3 garlic cloves
25 g/1 oz blanched almonds
1 large red pepper, deseeded and
   chopped roughly
1 tbsp ground cumin
2 tsp ground coriander
1 tsp ground turmeric
pinch of cayenne pepper
½ tsp salt
150 ml/5 fl oz water
3 star anise
2 tbsp lemon juice
pepper
flaked almonds, to garnish
rice, to serve

NUTRITION
Calories *421*; Sugars *5 g*; Protein *33 g*;
Carbohydrate *7 g*; Fat *30 g*; Saturates *6 g*

 moderate

20 mins

50 mins

1 Heat the butter and 1 tablespoon of the oil in a heavy-based frying pan. Add the chicken and cook for 5 minutes, until golden. Transfer the chicken to a plate and keep warm until required.

2 Combine the onion, ginger, garlic, almonds, red pepper, ground cumin, ground coriander, turmeric, cayenne pepper and salt in a food processor or liquidizer. Blend to form a smooth paste.

3 Heat the remaining oil in a large saucepan or deep frying pan. Add the spice paste and fry for 10–12 minutes.

4 Add the chicken, water, star anise, lemon juice and pepper. Reduce the heat, cover and simmer gently for 25 minutes, or until the chicken is tender, stirring a few times during cooking.

5 Transfer the chicken to a serving dish, sprinkle with the flaked almonds and serve with individual rice moulds.

Serve this fruity curry with mango chutney and naan bread. Mangoes or pears make a good substitute for the pineapple.

Chicken *and* Pineapple Curry

1 Heat the oil in a large, heavy-based frying pan. Coat the chicken in the seasoned flour and cook for about 4 minutes, until it has browned all over. Transfer the chicken to a large, deep casserole and keep warm until required.

2 Fry the shallots, garlic, apples, pineapple and sultanas over a low heat in the pan juices.

3 Add the honey, chicken stock, Worcestershire sauce and hot curry paste. Season with salt and pepper to taste.

4 Pour the sauce over the chicken and cover the casserole with a lid or cooking foil. Cook in the centre of a preheated oven, 180°C/350°F/Gas Mark 4, for about 2 hours. Stir in the soured cream and cook for a further 15 minutes. Garnish the curry with orange slices and serve with rice.

SERVES 4 – 6

1 tbsp oil
900 g/2 lb chicken meat, chopped
55 g/2 oz plain flour, seasoned
32 shallots, chopped roughly
4 garlic cloves, crushed with a little olive oil
3 cooking apples, cored and diced
1 pineapple, cored and diced
125 g/4½ oz sultanas
1 tbsp clear honey
300 ml/10 fl oz chicken stock
2 tbsp Worcestershire sauce
3 tbsp hot curry paste
150 ml/5 fl oz soured cream
salt and pepper
orange slices, to garnish
rice, to serve

NUTRITION
Calories *666*; Sugars *57 g*; Protein *57 g*;
Carbohydrate *72 g*; Fat *19 g*; Saturates *6 g*

 moderate

25 mins

 2 hrs 30 mins

COOK'S TIP

Coconut rice also makes an excellent accompaniment to this dish.

Serve these easy-to-prepare tortillas to friends or as a quick family supper. The chicken filling has a mild, mellow spicy heat and a fresh salad makes a perfect accompaniment.

Spicy Chicken Tortillas

SERVES 4

2 tbsp oil
8 skinless, boneless chicken thighs, sliced
1 onion, chopped
2 garlic cloves, chopped
1 tsp cumin seeds, crushed roughly
2 large dried chillies, sliced
400 g/14 oz canned tomatoes
400 g/14 oz canned red kidney beans,
    drained and rinsed
150 ml/5 fl oz chicken stock
2 tsp sugar
salt and pepper
lime wedges, to garnish

to serve

1 large, ripe avocado, stoned
1 lime
8 soft tortillas
250 ml/9 fl oz thick natural yogurt

NUTRITION
Calories *650*; Sugars *15 g*; Protein *48 g*;
Carbohydrate *47 g*; Fat *31 g*; Saturates *10 g*

 easy

10 mins

35 mins

1 Heat the oil in a large, heavy-based frying pan or preheated wok, add the chicken and fry for 3 minutes, until golden. Add the onion and fry for 5 minutes, stirring until browned. Add the garlic, cumin and chillies (with their seeds), and cook for about 1 minute.

2 Add the tomatoes, kidney beans, stock and sugar, and season with salt and pepper to taste. Bring to the boil, breaking up the tomatoes. Reduce the heat, cover and simmer for 15 minutes. Remove the lid and cook for 5 minutes, stirring occasionally until the sauce has thickened.

3 Scoop out the avocado flesh on to a plate and mash with a fork. Cut half of the lime into 8 thin wedges. Squeeze the juice from the remaining lime over the avocado.

4 Warm the tortillas according to the instructions on the packet. Put 2 tortillas on each serving plate, fill with the chicken mixture and top with spoonfuls of avocado and yogurt. Garnish the tortillas with lime wedges.

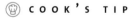

☻ **COOK'S TIP**

For a vegetarian filling, replace the chicken with 400 g/14 oz canned pinto or cannellini beans and use vegetable stock instead of the chicken stock.

This complete main course is cooked in one saucepan for simplicity. If you're cooking for one, simply halve the ingredients; the cooking time should stay the same.

One-pot Chicken

1 Heat the oil in a heavy-based frying pan and cook the chicken until golden. Remove the chicken from the pan using a slotted spoon. Stir in the onion, celery and green pepper and fry for 1 minute. Pour off any excess fat.

2 Add the rice and fry, stirring briskly, for a further minute. Add the chicken stock and heat until boiling.

3 Add the chilli and okra to the pan with the tomato purée. Season with salt and pepper to taste.

4 Return the chicken to the pan and stir. Cover tightly and simmer gently for 15 minutes, or until the rice is tender, the chicken is thoroughly cooked and all the liquid has been absorbed. Stir occasionally and if the mixture becomes too dry, add a little extra stock to moisten. Serve immediately.

SERVES 2

1 tbsp sunflower oil
4 chicken thighs
1 small onion, diced
2 celery sticks, diced
1 small green pepper, deseeded and diced
85 g/3 oz long-grain rice
300 ml/10 fl oz chicken stock
1 small red chilli, thinly sliced
250 g/9 oz okra
15 ml/1 tbsp tomato purée
salt and pepper

NUTRITION
Calories *425*; Sugars *8 g*; Protein *34 g*; Carbohydrate *48 g*; Fat *12 g*; Saturates *3 g*

⭐⭐ easy
◔ 10 mins
◕ 25 mins

 COOK'S TIP

You can replace the chicken with 250 g/9 oz peeled prawns and 85 g/3 oz belly of pork, if desired. Slice the pork and fry in the oil before adding the onions, and add the prawns 5 minutes before the end of the cooking time.

CHICKEN

Easy to put together, this dish makes a perfect mid-week supper. Use tortilla chips instead of baking the tortillas, if preferred.

Green Chilli *and* Chicken Chilaquiles

SERVES 4 – 6

12 stale tortillas, cut into strips
1 tbsp vegetable oil
1 small cooked chicken, meat removed from the bones and cut into bite-sized pieces
Salsa Verde (see below)
3 tbsp chopped fresh coriander
1 tsp finely chopped fresh oregano or thyme
4 garlic cloves, chopped finely
1/4 tsp ground cumin
350 g/12 oz grated cheese, such as Cheddar, manchego or mozzarella
450 ml/15 fl oz chicken stock
about 115 g/4 oz Parmesan cheese, grated

salsa verde

400g/14 oz green tomatoes, finely chopped
1-2 fresh green chillies, deseeded and chopped
1 green pepper, deseeded and chopped
1 small onion, chopped
1 bunch fresh coriander, chopped finely
1/2 tsp ground cumin

NUTRITION
Calories *682*; Sugars *1 g*; Protein *60 g*;
Carbohydrate *26 g*; Fat *38 g*; Saturates *20 g*

 easy

20 mins

 1 hr

1 Place the tortilla strips in a roasting tin, toss with the oil and bake in a preheated oven, 190°C/375°F/Gas Mark 5, for about 30 minutes until they are crisp and golden.

2 Combine the salsa ingredients in a bowl, adding salt to taste.

3 Arrange the chicken in a 23 x 33-cm/9 x 13-inch casserole, then sprinkle with half the salsa, coriander, oregano, garlic, cumin and some of the grated cheese. Repeat these layers and top with the tortilla strips.

4 Pour the stock over the top, then sprinkle with the remaining cheese.

5 Bake in the preheated oven for about 30 minutes, until heated through and the cheese is lightly golden.

COOK'S TIP

Serve garnished with crème fraîche or soured cream, thinly sliced spring onions, and a selection of pickled chillies.

Roasted garlic and mixed spices lend an evocative aroma to this tangy dish of simmered chicken, a speciality of Valladolid in Mexico's Yucatán peninsula.

Chicken *with* Yucatán Sauce

1 Place the chicken in a saucepan with enough stock to cover. Bring to the boil, then reduce the heat and simmer for 5 minutes. Remove from the heat and allow the chicken to cool in the stock; the chicken will continue to cook as it cools in the hot stock.

2 Meanwhile, roast the garlic cloves in an ungreased heavy-based frying pan until they are lightly browned on all sides and tender inside. Remove from the heat. When cool enough to handle, squeeze the flesh from the skins and place in a bowl.

3 Grind the garlic with the pepper, ground cloves, oregano, salt, lime juice and three-quarters of the cumin seeds. Mix with the flour.

4 When the chicken is cool, remove from the stock and pat dry. Reserve the stock. Rub the chicken with about two-thirds of the garlic-spice paste and stand at room temperature for 30 minutes, or overnight in the refrigerator.

5 Fry the onions and chillies in a little of the oil until golden brown and softened. Pour in the vinegar and remaining cumin seeds, cook for a few minutes, then add the reserved stock and remaining spice paste. Boil, stirring, for about 10 minutes, until reduced in volume.

6 Dredge the chicken in flour. Heat the remaining oil in a heavy-based frying pan. Fry the chicken until lightly browned, then remove from the pan and serve immediately, topped with the onion and vinegar sauce.

SERVES 4 – 6

8 small boned chicken thighs
chicken stock
15–20 garlic cloves, unpeeled
1 tsp coarsely ground black pepper
½ tsp ground cloves
2 tsp crumbled dried oregano or ½ tsp crushed or powdered bay leaves
about ½ tsp salt
1 tbsp lime juice
1 tsp cumin seeds, toasted lightly
1 tbsp flour, plus extra for dredging the chicken
3–4 onions, sliced thinly
2 fresh chillies, preferably mildish yellow ones, such as Mexican Guero or similar Turkish or Greek chillies, deseeded and sliced
120 ml/4 fl oz vegetable oil
100 ml/3½ fl oz cider or sherry vinegar

NUTRITION
Calories *313*; Sugars *6 g*; Protein *15 g*; Carbohydrate *14 g*; Fat *22 g*; Saturates *3 g*

 moderate

1 hr

25 mins

Chilli, tomatoes and
sweetcorn are typical
ingredients in
a Mexican dish.

Mexican Drumsticks

SERVES 4

2 tbsp oil
8 chicken drumsticks
1 onion, chopped finely
1 tsp chilli powder
1 tsp ground coriander
400 g/14 oz canned chopped tomatoes
2 tbsp tomato purée
125 g/4½ oz frozen sweetcorn
salt and pepper
rice and mixed pepper salad, to serve

1 Heat the oil in a large, heavy-based frying pan, add the chicken drumsticks and cook over a medium heat until lightly browned. Remove from the pan with a slotted spoon and set aside until required.

2 Add the onion to the pan and cook for 3–4 minutes, until softened, then stir in the chilli powder and coriander and cook for a few seconds, stirring briskly so the spices do not burn. Add the tomatoes and the tomato purée and stir well to combine.

3 Return the chicken drumsticks to the pan and simmer the casserole gently for 20 minutes, until the chicken is tender and thoroughly cooked. Add the sweetcorn and cook for a further 3–4 minutes. Season with salt and pepper.

4 Serve with the rice and mixed pepper salad.

NUTRITION
Calories *207*; Sugars *8 g*; Protein *18 g*;
Carbohydrate *13 g*; Fat *9 g*; Saturates *2 g*

 easy
5 mins
35 mins

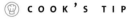 **COOK'S TIP**

Mexican dishes are not usually suitable for freezing because the strong flavours they contain, such as chilli, intensify during freezing, and if left for too long can result in an unpleasant, musty flavour.

This tasty chicken stir-fry is quick and easy to make and is full of fresh flavours and crunchy vegetables.

Chicken *with* Black Bean Sauce

1 Put the chicken in a bowl. Add the salt and cornflour and cover with water. Leave for 30 minutes.

2 Heat 1 tablespoon of the oil in a preheated wok or large, heavy-based frying pan and stir-fry the chicken for 4 minutes. Transfer the chicken to a warm serving dish and clean the wok or pan.

3 Add the remaining oil to the wok and add the garlic, black bean sauce, green and red peppers, chilli, mushrooms, onion and spring onions. Stir-fry the vegetables for 2 minutes, then return the chicken strips to the wok.

4 Add the seasoning, fry for 3 minutes and thicken with a little of the cornflour paste. Serve with fresh noodles.

SERVES 4

400 g/14 oz chicken breasts, sliced thinly
pinch of salt
pinch of cornflour
2 tbsp oil
1 garlic clove, crushed
1 tbsp black bean sauce
1 each small red and green pepper, deseeded and cut into strips
1 fresh red chilli, chopped finely
75 g/2¾ oz mushrooms, sliced
1 onion, chopped
6 spring onions, chopped
fresh noodles, to serve

seasoning
½ tsp salt
½ tsp sugar
3 tbsp chicken stock
1 tbsp dark soy sauce
2 tbsp beef stock
2 tbsp rice wine
1 tsp cornflour, blended with a little rice wine

NUTRITION
Calories 205; Sugars 4 g; Protein 25 g; Carbohydrate 6 g; Fat 9 g; Saturates 2 g

 moderate

40 mins

10 mins

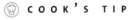 COOK'S TIP

Black bean sauce can be found in specialist shops and in many supermarkets. Use dried noodles, if you can't find fresh noodles.

The simple, Japanese style of cooking is ideal for thinly sliced chicken. Mirin is a rich, sweet rice wine which is available from Oriental shops.

Teppanyaki

SERVES 4

1 red pepper, deseeded and sliced thinly
1 green pepper, deseeded and sliced thinly
4 spring onions, sliced thinly
8 baby corn cobs, sliced thinly
100 g/3½ oz beansprouts
4 skinless, boneless chicken breasts, cut into
   5-mm/¼-inch diagonal slices
1 tbsp sesame or sunflower oil
4 tbsp soy sauce
4 tbsp mirin
1 tbsp grated fresh root ginger

1 Arrange the red and green peppers, spring onions, corn cobs and beansprouts on a plate with the chicken.

2 Heat a large griddle or heavy-based frying pan, then lightly brush with oil. Add the vegetables and chicken slices in small batches, allowing space between them so that they cook thoroughly.

3 In a small bowl, mix together the soy sauce, mirin and ginger and serve as a dip with the chicken and vegetables.

NUTRITION
Calories 206; Sugars 4 g; Protein 30 g;
Carbohydrate 6 g; Fat 7 g; Saturates 2 g

★★   easy
    10 mins
    10 mins

 COOK'S TIP

Instead of serving the sauce as a dip, you could use it as a marinade. However, do not leave the chicken to marinate for more than 2 hours as the soy sauce will cause it to dry out and become tough.

This exotic dish can be made with any cut of chicken, but drumsticks are best for quick and even cooking. Grated fresh coconut adds a delicious, tropical flavour.

Tropical Chicken

1 With a sharp knife, slash the chicken drumsticks at intervals, then place in a large bowl.

2 Sprinkle the lime juice over the chicken with the cayenne pepper. Cover and chill in the refrigerator for at least 2 hours or overnight.

3 Drain the chicken drumsticks using a slotted spoon and reserve the juice. Heat the oil in a heavy-based frying pan and sauté the chicken drumsticks, turning frequently, until golden. Stir in the marinade, lime rind, mango and the dark muscovado sugar.

4 Cover the pan and simmer gently, stirring occasionally, for 15 minutes, or until the juices run clear, not pink, when the chicken is pierced in the thickest part with a skewer. Garnish with lime wedges and fresh coriander.

SERVES 4

8 skinless chicken drumsticks
grated rind and juice of 2 limes
1 tsp cayenne pepper
1 tbsp sunflower oil
2 mangoes, stoned and sliced
2 tbsp dark muscovado sugar

to garnish
2 tbsp coarsely grated coconut
lime wedges
sprigs of fresh coriander

NUTRITION
Calories *283*; Sugars *21 g*; Protein *24 g*; Carbohydrate *21 g*; Fat *12 g*; Saturates *3 g*

⭐⭐   easy
         2 hrs 20 mins
         30 mins

🧑‍🍳 **COOK'S TIP**

When buying mangoes, bear in mind that the skin of ripe mangoes varies in colour from green to pinky-red and the flesh from pale yellow to bright orange. Choose mangoes which yield to gentle pressure.

This unusual dish, with its mixture of chicken and shellfish, is typically Spanish. The basis of this recipe is a *sofrito*, a slow-cooked mixture of onion and tomato in olive oil, with garlic and peppers.

Chicken *and* Chorizo *with* Prawns

SERVES 4

1 tbsp olive oil
4 chicken quarters
1 red pepper, deseeded and sliced
1 onion, sliced
2 garlic cloves, crushed
400 g/14 oz canned chopped tomatoes
200 ml/7 fl oz dry white wine
4 tbsp chopped fresh oregano
125 g/4½ oz chorizo sausage, thinly sliced
125 g/4½ oz peeled cooked prawns
salt and pepper
plain rice, to serve

1 Heat the oil in a heavy-based frying pan and cook the chicken, turning occasionally until golden brown.

2 Add the pepper and onion to the pan and fry gently until softened.

3 Add the garlic with the tomatoes, wine and oregano. Season with salt and pepper to taste, then bring to the boil. Reduce the heat, cover and simmer gently for 45 minutes, or until the chicken is tender and the juices run clear, not pink, when the chicken is pierced in the thickest part with a skewer.

4 Add the chorizo to the pan with the prawns, then simmer for a further 5 minutes. Adjust the seasoning to taste and serve with the rice.

NUTRITION
Calories *470*; Sugars *9 g*; Protein *52 g*;
Carbohydrate *10 g*; Fat *21 g*; Saturates *6 g*

easy

20 mins

1 hr

🍳 **COOK'S TIP**

Chorizo is a spicy Spanish sausage made with pork and a hot pepper, such as cayenne or pimento. It is available from most large supermarkets and specialist butchers.

For this very popular dish, small pieces of chicken are marinated in a creamy mixture of yogurt, garlic and spices.

Spicy Grilled Chicken Tikka

1 Blend together the ginger, garlic, ground coriander, ground cumin and chilli powder in a large mixing bowl.

2 Add the yogurt, salt, lemon juice, red food colouring (if using), and the tomato purée to the spice mixture.

3 Add the chicken to the spice mixture and toss to coat well. Leave to marinate in the refrigerator for at least 3 hours, preferably overnight.

4 Arrange the onion in the bottom of a heatproof dish. Carefully drizzle half of the oil over the onions.

5 Arrange the marinated chicken pieces on top of the onions and cook under a pre-heated medium-hot grill, turning once and basting with the remaining oil, for 25-30 minutes.

6 Serve garnished with the lemon wedges on a bed of lettuce.

SERVES 6

1 tsp fresh root ginger, chopped finely
1 tsp fresh garlic, crushed
½ tsp ground coriander
½ tsp ground cumin
1 tsp chilli powder
3 tbsp natural yogurt
1 tsp salt
2 tbsp lemon juice
few drops of red food colouring (optional)
1 tbsp tomato purée
1.5 kg/3 lb 5 oz chicken breasts, cut into bite-sized pieces
1 onion, sliced
3 tbsp oil
1 lemon, cut into wedges, to garnish

NUTRITION
Calories *173*; Sugars *6 g*; Protein *28 g*; Carbohydrate *6 g*; Fat *4 g*; Saturates *2 g*

easy

3 hrs 20 mins

30 mins

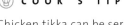 COOK'S TIP

Chicken tikka can be served with naan bread, chutney and raita, which is a mixture of chopped garlic, cucumber and natural yogurt.

This is a quick and tasty way to use leftover roast chicken. The sauce can also be used for other types of cooked meat, such as poultry, lamb or beef.

Fragrant Chicken *and* Broad Beans

SERVES 4

1 tsp mustard oil
3 tbsp vegetable oil
1 large onion, chopped finely
3 garlic cloves, crushed
1 tbsp tomato purée
2 tomatoes, peeled and chopped
1 tsp ground turmeric
½ tsp ground cumin
½ tsp ground coriander
½ tsp chilli powder
½ tsp garam masala
1 tsp red wine vinegar
1 small red pepper, deseeded and chopped
125 g/4 oz frozen broad beans
500 g/1 lb cooked chicken breasts, cut into bite-sized pieces
salt
sprigs of fresh coriander, to garnish

1 Heat the mustard oil in a large, heavy-based frying pan over a high heat for about 1 minute, until it begins to smoke. Add the vegetable oil and reduce the heat. Add the onion and the garlic and cook until golden.

2 Add the tomato purée, tomatoes, ground turmeric, ground cumin and ground coriander, chilli powder, garam masala and red wine vinegar to the frying pan. Stir well until fragrant.

3 Add the red pepper and broad beans and stir for 2 minutes, until the pepper has softened. Stir in the chicken and season with salt to taste. Simmer gently for 6–8 minutes, until the chicken is heated through and the broad beans are tender.

4 Serve garnished with sprigs of coriander.

NUTRITION
Calories 270; Sugars 3 g; Protein 36 g; Carbohydrate 7 g; Fat 11 g; Saturates 2 g

easy
20 mins
20 mins

 **COOK'S TIP**

This dish is an ideal way of using up leftover poultry – turkey, duck or quail. Any variety of bean works well, but vegetables are just as good, especially root vegetables, courgettes, potatoes or broccoli.

This biryani recipe may look rather complicated, but is not difficult to follow. You can substitute lamb for the chicken.

Chicken Biryani

1 Blend together the ginger, garlic, garam masala, chilli powder, ground turmeric, 1 teaspoon salt and cardamom seeds and mix with the yogurt and chicken pieces. Set aside to marinate for 3 hours.

2 Pour the milk into a pan and bring to the boil. Pour it over the saffron and set aside.

3 Heat the ghee in a large, heavy-based saucepan. Cook the onions until golden. Set aside.

4 Place the rice, cinnamon sticks, peppercorns and black cumin seeds in a pan of water. Bring the rice to the boil and remove from the heat when half-cooked. Drain and place in a bowl. Mix with the remaining salt.

5 Add the chicken mixture to the pan with the onions and ghee. Add the chillies, coriander, lemon juice and saffron. Add the rice, cover tightly and cook over a low heat for 1 hour. Check that the meat is cooked through before serving. If the meat is not cooked, return to the heat and cook for a further 15 minutes. Mix thoroughly before serving hot.

SERVES 4

1½ tsp finely chopped fresh root ginger
1½ tsp crushed fresh garlic
1 tbsp garam masala
1 tsp chilli powder
½ tsp ground turmeric
2 tsp salt
20 green/white cardamom seeds, crushed
300 ml/10 fl oz natural yogurt
1.5 kg/3 lb 5 oz chicken, skinned and cut into 8 pieces
150 ml/5 fl oz milk
saffron strands
6 tbsp ghee
2 onions, sliced
450 g/1 lb basmati rice, rinsed
2 cinnamon sticks
4 black peppercorns
1 tsp black cumin seeds
4 fresh green chillies, chopped finely
1 tbsp chopped fresh coriander
4 tbsp lemon juice

NUTRITION
Calories 382; Sugars 8 g; Protein 42 g; Carbohydrate 10 g; Fat 20 g; Saturates 11 g

  moderate
3 hrs 20 mins
1 hr 30 mins

In India, tandoori chicken is traditionally cooked in a tandoor oven but a grill produces a similarly delicious result.

Grilled Tandoori Chicken

SERVES 4

8 skinless chicken drumsticks
150 ml/5 fl oz natural yogurt
1½ tsp finely chopped fresh root ginger
1½ tsp crushed fresh garlic
1 tsp chilli powder
2 tsp ground cumin
2 tsp ground coriander
1 tsp salt
½ tsp red food colouring
1 tbsp tamarind paste
150 ml/5 fl oz water
150 ml/5 fl oz oil

to serve
lettuce leaves
onion rings
lemon wedges
naan bread

NUTRITION
Calories 514; Sugars 5 g; Protein 28 g;
Carbohydrate 6 g; Fat 43 g; Saturates 6 g

easy
6 hrs 30 mins
35 mins

1 Make 2–3 slashes in each piece of chicken.

2 Place the yogurt in a bowl. Add the ginger, garlic, chilli powder, ground cumin, ground coriander, salt and red food colouring and blend together until well combined.

3 Add the chicken to the yogurt mixture and mix to coat well. Leave the chicken to marinate in the refrigerator for a minimum of 3 hours.

4 In a separate bowl, mix the tamarind paste with the water and fold into the yogurt mixture. Toss the chicken pieces in this mixture and set aside to marinate for a further 3 hours.

5 Transfer the chicken pieces to a heatproof dish and brush the chicken with oil. Cook the chicken under a preheated medium-hot grill for 30–35 minutes, turning the chicken pieces occasionally and basting with the remaining oil.

6 Arrange the chicken on a bed of lettuce and onion, and serve with lemon wedges and naan bread.

 COOK'S TIP

A cooling raita of chopped garlic, cucumber and natural yogurt will complement this dish perfectly.

Korma is a typically mild, aromatic curry. If you want to reduce the fat in this recipe, use natural yogurt instead of the cream.

Chicken Korma *with* Coriander

1 Place the ingredients for the korma paste into a blender or food processor and blend together to make a very smooth paste.

2 Place the chicken in a bowl and spoon the korma paste over. Stir to coat the chicken completely with the paste. Cover and chill in the refrigerator for 3 hours to allow the flavours to permeate the chicken.

3 Simmer the meat in a large saucepan for 25 minutes, adding a little chicken stock if the mixture becomes too dry.

4 Add the double cream and garam masala to the pan and simmer for a further 15 minutes. Allow the korma to stand for 10 minutes before serving. Garnish the chicken korma with coriander and serve with rice.

SERVES 6

750 g/1 lb 10 oz chicken meat, cut into bite-sized pieces
300 ml/10 fl oz double cream
½ tsp garam masala

korma paste

2 garlic cloves
2.5-cm/1-inch piece of fresh root ginger, chopped coarsely
50 g/1¾ oz blanched almonds
6 tbsp chicken stock
1 tsp ground cardamon
4 cloves, crushed
1 tsp cinnamon
2 large onions, chopped
1 tsp coriander seeds
2 tsp ground cumin
pinch of cayenne
6 tbsp olive oil
salt and pepper
sprigs of fresh coriander, to garnish
plain rice, to serve

NUTRITION

Calories *488*; Sugars *6 g*; Protein *21 g*; Carbohydrate *9 g*; Fat *42 g*; Saturates *17 g*

✪✪✪ moderate
🕐 3 hrs 40 mins
🕐 40 mins

 COOK'S TIP

To prepare your own garam masala, grind 1 teaspoon cardamon seeds with 2 teaspoons cloves, 2 tablespoons each cumin and coriander seeds, 1 cinnamon stick, 1 tablespoon black peppercorns and 1 dried red chilli.

This spicy roast chicken is accompanied by a flavourful stuffing, including rice, garlic, cashew nuts and ginger.

Roast Chicken *with* Cashew Nuts

SERVES 4

1 chicken, weighing about 1.5 kg/3 lb 5 oz
1 small onion, halved
25 g/1 oz butter, melted
1 tsp ground turmeric
1 tsp ground ginger
½ tsp cayenne
salt and pepper
sprigs of fresh coriander, to garnish

stuffing

2 tbsp oil
1 onion, chopped finely
½ red pepper, deseeded and chopped finely
2 garlic cloves, crushed
125 g/4½ oz basmati rice, rinsed
350 ml/12 fl oz hot chicken stock
grated rind of ½ lemon
½ tsp ground turmeric
½ tsp ground ginger
½ tsp ground coriander
pinch cayenne pepper
85 g/3 oz salted cashew nuts

NUTRITION

Calories *587*; Sugars *5 g*; Protein *52 g*;
Carbohydrate *35 g*; Fat *26 g*; Saturates *8 g*

moderate

30 mins

2 hrs

1 To make the stuffing, heat the oil in a heavy-based saucepan. Add the onion, red pepper and garlic and cook gently for 4–5 minutes. Add the rice and stir to coat in the oil. Add the stock, bring to the boil, then simmer for 15 minutes, until all of the liquid has been absorbed. Transfer to a bowl and add the remaining ingredients for the stuffing. Season with pepper to taste.

2 Place half of the stuffing in the neck end of the chicken with the onion and secure with a cocktail stick. Spoon the rest of the rice stuffing into a greased ovenproof dish and cover with foil.

3 Place the chicken in a roasting tin. Prick all over avoiding the stuffed area. Mix together the butter and spices, season, then brush the mixture over the chicken.

4 Roast in a preheated oven, 190°C/375°F/Gas Mark 5, for 1 hour, basting from time to time. Place the dish of rice stuffing in the oven and continue cooking the chicken for 30 minutes. Remove the cocktail stick and serve the chicken with the stuffing, garnished with sprigs of coriander.

The intense flavours of this dish are helped by the slow, gentle cooking. The meat should be almost falling off the bone.

Braised Garlic Chicken

1 Place the garlic, shallots, chillies, lemon grass, coriander and shrimp paste in a pestle and mortar and grind to an almost smooth paste. Stir in the cinnamon and tamarind paste.

2 Heat the oil in a large, heavy-based frying pan or preheated wok. Add the chicken joints, turning frequently, until they are golden brown on all sides. Remove them from the pan with a draining spoon and keep hot. Tip away any excess fat.

3 Add the garlic paste to the pan and cook over a medium heat, stirring constantly, until lightly browned. Stir in the stock and return the chicken to the pan.

4 Bring to the boil, cover, reduce the heat and simmer, stirring occasionally, for 25–30 minutes, until the chicken is tender and thoroughly cooked. Stir in the fish sauce and peanut butter and simmer for a further 10 minutes.

5 Season with salt and pepper to taste and sprinkle the toasted peanuts over the chicken. Serve immediately with the stir-fried vegetables and noodles.

SERVES 4

4 garlic cloves, chopped
4 shallots, chopped
2 small fresh red chillies, deseeded and chopped
1 lemon grass stalk, outer leaves removed and chopped finely
1 tbsp chopped fresh coriander
1 tsp shrimp paste
½ tsp ground cinnamon
1 tbsp tamarind paste
2 tbsp vegetable oil
8 small chicken joints, such as drumsticks or thighs
300 ml/10 fl oz chicken stock
1 tbsp Thai fish sauce
1 tbsp smooth peanut butter
4 tbsp chopped toasted peanuts
salt and pepper
stir-fried vegetables and noodles, to serve

NUTRITION
Calories 282; Sugars 3 g; Protein 29 g; Carbohydrate 5 g; Fat 16 g; Saturates 3 g

✪✪✪   moderate

     15 mins

     1 hr

Coconut adds a creamy texture and delicious flavour to this Thai-style stir-fry, which is spiked with green chilli.

Chilli Coconut Chicken

SERVES 4

3 tbsp sesame oil
350 g/12 oz chicken breasts, sliced thinly
8 shallots, sliced
2 garlic cloves, chopped finely
2.5-cm/1-inch piece of fresh root ginger, grated
1 fresh green chilli, chopped finely
1 each red and green pepper, deseeded and sliced thinly
3 courgettes, sliced thinly
2 tbsp ground almonds
1 tsp ground cinnamon
1 tbsp oyster sauce
50 g/1¾ oz creamed coconut, grated
salt and pepper

1 Heat the sesame oil in a preheated wok or large, heavy-based frying pan. Add the chicken, season with salt and pepper to taste, and stir-fry for about 4 minutes.

2 Add the shallots, garlic, ginger and chilli and stir-fry for a further 2 minutes.

3 Add the peppers and courgettes and cook for about 1 minute.

4 Add the remaining ingredients and adjust the seasoning. Stir-fry for 1 minute and serve.

NUTRITION
Calories *184*; Sugars *6 g*; Protein *24 g*; Carbohydrate *8 g*; Fat *5 g*; Saturates *2 g*

 easy

15 mins

10 mins

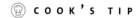 COOK'S TIP

Creamed coconut is sold in blocks in supermarkets and Oriental stores. It is a useful store-cupboard standby as it adds richness and depth of flavour.

These simple marinated chicken portions are packed with powerful, zesty flavours, best accompanied by plain rice and a cucumber salad.

Spicy Coriander Chicken

1 Using a sharp knife, cut 3 deep slashes down the side of each chicken breast. Place them in a single layer in a wide, non-metallic dish.

2 Put the garlic, chilli, ginger, coriander, lime rind and juice, soy sauce, caster sugar and coconut milk in a food processor and process to a smooth purée.

3 Spread the purée over both sides of the chicken portions, coating them evenly. Cover the dish with clingfilm and set aside to marinate in the refrigerator for about 1 hour.

4 Lift the chicken from the marinade, drain off the excess and place in a grill pan. Cook under a preheated grill for 12–15 minutes, until thoroughly and evenly cooked.

5 Meanwhile, place the remaining marinade in a saucepan and bring to the boil. Reduce the heat and simmer for several minutes to heat thoroughly. Remove the pan from the heat.

6 Place the chicken breast portions on warm serving plates and pour the sauce over. Serve immediately accompanied with rice and the cucumber and radish salad.

SERVES 4

4 skinless, boneless chicken breasts
2 garlic cloves, peeled
1 fresh green chilli, deseeded
2-cm/3/4-inch piece of fresh root ginger, chopped
4 tbsp chopped fresh coriander
finely grated rind of 1 lime
3 tbsp lime juice
2 tbsp light soy sauce
1 tbsp caster sugar
175 ml/6 fl oz coconut milk

to serve
plain rice
cucumber and radish salad

NUTRITION
Calories 171; Sugars 8 g; Protein 31 g;
Carbohydrate 9 g; Fat 2 g; Saturates 0.5 g

    moderate
    1 hr 25 mins
         20 mins

This quick dish has many variations, but this version includes the classic combination of peanuts, chicken and chillies, blending together to give an aromatic dish.

Chilli *and* Peanut Chicken

SERVES 4

2 tbsp groundnut oil
125 g/4½ oz shelled peanuts
300 g/10½ oz skinless, boneless chicken breasts, cut into 2.5-cm/1-inch cubes
1 fresh red chilli, sliced
1 green pepper, deseeded and cut into strips
fried rice, to serve

sauce
150 ml/5 fl oz chicken stock
1 tbsp Chinese rice wine or dry sherry
1 tbsp light soy sauce
1½ tsp light brown sugar
2 garlic cloves, crushed
1 tsp grated fresh root ginger
1 tsp rice wine vinegar
1 tsp sesame oil

1 Heat the peanut oil in a preheated wok or large, heavy-based frying pan. Add the peanuts and stir-fry for 1 minute. Remove the peanuts with a slotted spoon and set aside.

2 Add the chicken to the wok and cook for 1–2 minutes. Stir in the chilli and green pepper and cook for 1 minute. Remove from the wok with a slotted spoon and set aside.

3 Put half of the peanuts in a food processor and process until almost smooth. Alternatively, place them in a plastic bag and crush them with a rolling pin.

4 To make the sauce, add the chicken stock, Chinese rice wine, soy sauce, sugar, garlic, ginger and rice wine vinegar to the wok.

5 Heat the sauce without boiling and stir in the peanuts, chicken, chilli and green pepper.

6 Sprinkle the sesame oil into the wok, stir and cook for 1 minute. Serve hot with fried rice.

NUTRITION
Calories *324*; Sugars *3 g*; Protein *25 g*; Carbohydrate *6 g*; Fat *24 g*; Saturates *5 g*

moderate

15 mins

10 mins

🎩 COOK'S TIP

If necessary, process the peanuts with a little of the stock in step 4 to make a softer paste.

This is a simple version
of a creamy textured and
mildly spiced Indian pilau.

Indian Chicken *and* Sultana Pilau

1 Heat the butter in a heavy-based saucepan and fry the chicken with the onion for about 3 minutes.

2 Stir in the ground turmeric, ground cinnamon, rice and fry gently for 3 minutes.

3 Add the yogurt, sultanas and chicken stock and mix well. Cover and simmer for 10 minutes, stirring occasionally, until the rice is tender and the stock has been absorbed. Add more stock if the mixture becomes too dry.

4 Stir in the tomato and coriander. Sprinkle the pilau with the toasted coconut and garnish with fresh coriander.

SERVES 4

60 g/2 oz butter
8 skinless, boneless chicken thighs, cut into large pieces
1 onion, sliced
1 tsp ground turmeric
1 tsp ground cinnamon
250 g/9 oz long-grain rice
425 ml/15 fl oz natural yogurt
55 g/2 oz sultanas
200 ml/7 fl oz chicken stock
1 tomato, chopped
2 tbsp chopped fresh coriander or parsley
2 tbsp toasted coconut
salt and pepper
sprigs of fresh coriander, to garnish

NUTRITION
Calories 581; Sugars 22 g; Protein 31 g; Carbohydrate 73 g; Fat 19 g; Saturates 12 g

 easy
 10 mins
10 mins
25 mins

 COOK'S TIP

Long-grain rice is the most widely available, although basmati, with its slender grains, has a more aromatic flavour. Rice, especially basmati, should be washed thoroughly under cold, running water before use.

This warming, rich and spicy dish is based on the traditional cooking style of Northern India, using chicken on the bone.

Spiced Chicken *with* Pilau Rice

SERVES 4

4 skinless chicken drumsticks
4 skinless chicken thighs
150 ml/5 fl oz natural yogurt
4 tbsp tikka curry paste
2 tbsp sunflower oil
1 onion, sliced thinly
1 garlic clove, crushed
1 tsp ground cumin
1 tsp finely chopped fresh root ginger
½ tsp chilli paste
4 tsp chicken stock
2 tbsp ground almonds
salt
sprigs of fresh coriander, to garnish

to serve
pilau rice
pickles
poppadums

NUTRITION
Calories *276*; Sugars *6 g*; Protein *28 g*;
Carbohydrate *8 g*; Fat *15 g*; Saturates *3 g*

 ⭐⭐⭐ moderate
🕐 1 hr 15 mins
🕐 35 mins

1 Using a sharp knife, slash the chicken drumsticks and thighs fairly deeply at intervals and place in a large bowl.

2 Mix together the yogurt and curry paste and stir into the chicken, tossing to coat evenly. Cover and chill for at least 1 hour.

3 Heat the oil in a large, heavy-based saucepan. Add the onion and garlic and cook for 4–5 minutes, until softened but not browned.

4 Stir in the ground cumin, ginger and chilli paste and cook gently for 1 minute.

5 Add the chicken pieces and fry gently, turning from time to time, for about 10 minutes, or until evenly browned. Stir in any remaining marinade with the stock and almonds.

6 Cover the pan and simmer gently for a further 15 minutes, or until the chicken is completely cooked and tender.

7 Season with salt to taste. Garnish the chicken with coriander and serve with pilau rice, pickles and poppadums.

🍳 COOK'S TIP

Use boneless chicken breasts instead of legs, and cut into large chunks for cooking, if preferred.

Spiced chicken legs are partially boned and packed with dried apricots for an intense fruity flavour. A golden, low-fat yogurt coating keeps the chicken moist and tender.

Lemon *and* Apricot Chicken

1 Use a small sharp knife carefully to cut the flesh away from the thigh bone. Scrape the meat away down as far as the knuckle. Grasp the thigh bone firmly and twist it to break it away from the drumstick.

2 Open out the boned part of the chicken and sprinkle with the lemon rind and season with pepper to taste. Pack the dried apricots into each piece of chicken. Fold over to enclose and secure with cocktail sticks.

3 Mix together the ground cumin, ground turmeric and yogurt, and season with salt and pepper to taste. Brush the mixture over the chicken to coat evenly. Place the chicken in an ovenproof dish or roasting tin and bake in a preheated oven, 190°C/375°F/Gas Mark 5, for about 35–40 minutes, or until the juices run clear, not pink, when the chicken is pierced through the thickest part with a skewer.

4 Meanwhile, cook the rice in boiling, lightly salted water until just tender, then drain well. Stir the toasted hazelnuts and sunflower seeds into the rice. Serve the chicken with the nutty rice, lemon wedges and a green salad.

SERVES 4

4 large, skinless chicken leg quarters
finely grated rind of 1 lemon
200 g/7 oz ready-to-eat dried apricots
1 tbsp ground cumin
1 tsp ground turmeric
125 g/4½ oz low-fat natural yogurt
salt and pepper

to serve
250 g/9 oz brown rice
2 tbsp flaked hazelnuts or almonds, toasted
2 tbsp sunflower seeds, toasted
lemon wedges
green salad

NUTRITION
Calories *305*; Sugars *21 g*; Protein *15 g*;
Carbohydrate *45 g*; Fat *8 g*; Saturates *1 g*

 moderate

 20 mins

20 mins

40 mins

This is a popular and attractive dinner party dish. It should ideally be cooked and served from a karahi, but if you do not have one a deep, heavy-based frying pan will do.

Herbed Chicken *with* Vegetables

SERVES 4

8 chicken drumsticks
1½ tsp finely chopped fresh root ginger
1½ tsp crushed fresh garlic
1 tsp salt
2 onions, chopped
½ large bunch of fresh coriander leaves
4–6 fresh green chillies
600 ml/1 pint oil
4 firm tomatoes, cut into wedges
2 large green peppers, deseeded and
   chopped roughly

1 Make 2–3 slashes in each piece of chicken. Rub the ginger, garlic and salt over the chicken pieces and set aside.

2 Place half of the onions, the coriander leaves and green chillies in a pestle and mortar and grind to a paste. Rub the paste over the chicken pieces.

3 Heat the oil in a preheated karahi or large, heavy-based frying pan over a high heat. Add the remaining onions and fry until golden brown. Remove the onions from the pan with a slotted spoon and set aside.

4 Reduce the heat to medium and fry the chicken in batches for 5–7 minutes per batch, until cooked through. Drain on kitchen paper and keep warm.

5 Add the tomatoes and the peppers to the pan and half-cook them until they are softened but still have 'bite'.

6 Transfer the tomatoes and green peppers to a serving plate and arrange the chicken on top. Garnish with the reserved fried onions.

NUTRITION
Calories *499*; Sugars *10 g*; Protein *33 g*;
Carbohydrate *12 g*; Fat *36 g*; Saturates *6 g*

easy

20 mins

45 mins

This tasty Thai-style dish has a classic sauce of lime, peanut, coconut and chilli. You'll find coconut cream in most supermarkets or delicatessens.

Thai Coconut Chicken

1 Place the chicken stock in a measuring jug and crumble the creamed coconut into the stock, stirring to dissolve.

2 Heat the oil in a preheated wok or large, heavy-based frying pan and cook the chicken strips, stirring, until golden.

3 Add the red chilli and the spring onions to the wok and cook gently for a few minutes, stirring until combined.

4 Add the peanut butter, coconut cream mixture, lime rind and juice and simmer uncovered, stirring, for about 5 minutes.

5 Serve with rice, garnished with spring onion flowers and red chillies.

SERVES 4

150 ml/5 fl oz hot chicken stock
25 g/1 oz coconut cream
1 tbsp sunflower oil
8 skinless, boneless chicken thighs, cut into long, thin strips
1 small fresh red chilli, sliced thinly
4 spring onions, sliced thinly
4 tbsp smooth or crunchy peanut butter
finely grated rind and juice of 1 lime
plain rice, to serve

to garnish
spring onion 'flowers'
red chillies

NUTRITION
Calories *348*; Sugars *2 g*; Protein *36 g*; Carbohydrate *3 g*; Fat *21 g*; Saturates *8 g*

⭐⭐   easy
🍳   10 mins
🕐   15 mins

🧑‍🍳 **COOK'S TIP**

Limes are used frequently in Thai cookery, particularly in conjunction with sweet flavours such as coconut.

Index